D1739324

Special Thanks:

Steve Hergenrader

Deby Hergenrader

Pat Sims

Terra Lynch

Jared Hergenrader

Tyler Hergenrader

Peter Matthews

Mullen/Stewart/Hergenrader Family

Life Of
A Trailblazer

CARMEL MULLEN

100 Year Legacy

A Life Lived Out

STORY ONE

Water

Water is so powerful with the waves, storms, floods, tsunamis, sleet and snow. Water grows food for life which would not be possible without it. I think about how important water is and how we can't live without it. We drink it. We bathe in it. We wash our clothes, our dishes and utensils, and cook with it. It can be cold, hot, warm, icy, tasty, runny, stagnant, muddy, or salty. It can come from so many places—rain, oceans, rivers, creeks, wells, and springs.

Water can also be used for pleasure, like ice skating, hockey, swimming and diving and other activities. One hot, summer day, a group of my friends from the Ice Capades decided to go to this huge, beautiful, popular pool. We were swimming and diving and playing around. We were having fun playing tag and Marco Polo. Someone said "let's play Follow the Leader." So we did. More and more people joined our group. We jumped off the side, did cannon balls and somersaults into the water, swam underwater, and dove off the diving board. We seemed to take over the pool. We decided to play "Stump the Leader."

If you couldn't do the trick you had to drop out of the game. We did harder tricks like swan dives, jackknives and back dives off of the low board. Fewer people were left in the game. It became competitive and got harder. My turn came to become the "leader". I decided to do a handstand off of the high board. As I climbed the ladder, I just knew that all eyes were on me. I felt so proud. I approached the end of the board. I stood erect, posed, held a perfect handstand with pointed toes for a moment, pushed off, and entered the water with hardly a ripple. I dove deep and as I swam to the surface I just knew I had done a perfect dive. Yes, there was a huge applause as I broke water. But everyone was laughing. Why? I laughed with them. I looked around and then I knew why. Floating nearby were my falsies. They must have popped out of my bathing suit during the dive. I was so embarrassed. They beat me to the surface.

STORY TWO

A Night I Will Never Forget

It's opening night for the Ice Capades Ice Show ... 1949 ... Empress Hall, London, England.

I checked in at the Ice Capades door at 7:00. If we were late, we would be fined $1.00 per minute. I went to the dressing room, applied my makeup, laced up my boots, and put on my headdress. I also had on pantaloon pants. I was then ready to step into my beautiful, elegant dress for the opening number. The dress had been laid out on the floor for me to step into it. It was a Dresden doll dress with a huge skirt and a wooden hoop around the bottom. The dress was made of satin and lace and loads of shiny sequins. The dress had a zipper down the back, so I stepped over the hoop and into the dress. A "dresser", or helper, then zipped me up and I was ready to perform.

I heard the two minute call. The show was about ready to start. I rushed backstage to line up for our entrance. The overture was playing. The lights were off so we rushed to our places on the ice in the dark.

Our music and the lights came on together. We started our dance down the ice. We heard a tremendous applause as the light hit our dresses. All of a sudden, I stubbed my toe, and fell. My hoop flipped over my head. I fell to the ice. I was like a bug on its back, trying to find the ice. My legs were straight up in the air. My partner tried to help but I couldn't even turn over. One of the stage hands came out. I was lying on the zipper. The rest of the dance continued. I still struggled. Finally there was a blackout and they dragged me off the ice by my hoop. What an embarrassing circus that turned out to be!

STORY THREE

A Lesson Learned

Have you ever been accused of stealing and you really didn't do it? Oh boy, I was in Toronto, Canada, in the early 40's with the Ice Capades Ice Show and we were called in for an early morning dress rehearsal. You couldn't depend on the bus service so a group of us decided to take a cab.

I couldn't find my comb and had to borrow my roommate's before going to breakfast. I asked our group if we could stop at Simpson's Department Store on the way. I knew where the notions counter was so it wouldn't take long for me to run in, pick up a comb, pay for it and be back in no time. A comb is so important because we had hair wigs to change in the show and everyone needed to use their own. They said "okay, but hurry because we will be fined $1.00 a minute ifwe are late."

The cab pulled up pretty close to the door so I jumped out and ran in. It had snowed that night so I had to be careful because the walkway was covered over with a slick sheet of slushy ice. I ran inside over to the notions counter and found a comb.

There were quite a few people around but I had my dime in my hand so I picked one up and showed it to the clerk. I gave her my dime and said "don't bother wrapping it up, I'll put it in my purse because I'm in a hurry." In those days when you bought something the clerk would put the item in a basket with your money. The basket would then be on a pulley that took it up to the mezzanine where another worker would wrap it, make change, tie it with string and then send it all back to you in the basket. I was in a hurry so I thought it would take too long. I was thinking of all the fines we would be getting and my name would be "mud" along with my skating friends. I started to leave and got almost to the exit door when this man grabbed me by the shoulder. I stopped and he said "We don't do things like that here!"

"What did I do?"

"Where did you get that comb?"

"From the notions counter-I paid the clerk for it."

He said, "You show me who you got it from."

I did, but the clerk said she could have, but she'd been so busy with the Christmas rush she just couldn't remember me.

I said, "I did pay for it."

He then said, "You come with me!"

He took me up to the mezzanine where a big man was sitting at a huge desk. He started to lecture me about how at first you steal the little things, then the bigger things ... then you are in big trouble. I was thinking of the cab meter going up, the fines and my friends waiting for me so I threw the comb on his desk, saying "I did pay for it!" and ran down the stairs. I almost got to the door when the same man grabbed me by the shoulder which spun me around and I fell flat on the floor. Instead of picking me up like any gentleman would do, he started pulling my leg ...just like I'm pulling yours!

STORY FOUR

My Dad

My dad was the supervisor for several logging camps and saw-mills in Michigan's Upper Peninsula. He loved the woods and would work in the woods all week, then come home to his family on Friday night. He would then leave for camp early Monday morning. Our family consisted of mom and dad and five kids-four girls and one boy. I was the youngest. We lived in a small town called Newberry, Michigan.

Dad always came home with something from the woods for us kids. His pockets could be filled with shelled beechnuts from a squirrel's nest, a pail of honey and the comb from a bee's nest, or wild berries he picked along the river. At Christmas time, he would take us through the snow and woods and cut the most beautiful pine tree, and then have us drag it to our car and home. If it wasn't perfect he would bore a hole in the trunk and add another branch.

He'd take us camping often-usually near a river or lake. We would pitch our tent and then go fishing for rainbow trout or speckled brown trout. Legally the trout had to be 8" long and 12 would be your limit. If the fish were too small, dad called them "finger food", and he would hide them in the fingers of his gloves and we would cook them for dinner that night. Other times he would take us to a special place where he had his fish spears hidden under a log and he would teach us how the Indians speared their fish.

Sometimes the camps were near the railroad tracks so when dad let us visit he arranged it so we could ride in the little red caboose. Other times we would ride on the "speeder" or "peed" as dad called it. It was like a golf cart. Two men would push and pull a bar back and forth, pumping us down the track. When we arrived we would run to the cook house and find the huge cookie barrel where we could eat as many as we wanted. If it was lunch or dinner time, the cook would let us blow the long dinner horn that called the men to eat. The tables were long and every 5' was a table setting of plates, cups, silverware, milk, sugar, salt, pepper, food for the meal and a huge coffee pot. No one could talk. Everything was within reach so they could help themselves, eat and leave. The "cookie", or cook's helper, and the cook had to start on the next meal. They had to clean up the dishes, butcher the meat, cut it up, etc. They had no refrigeration-just the ice house or cellar to keep things cold. They also had to keep the fire going for cooking, baking and keeping the water hot.

During the Depression, we did the laundry for the lumber-jacks. Dad brought bags of it in on the train. We kids would meet the train, load the bags on our sled or wagon, and take it home. Mom washed it. We kids hung it on the clothesline to dry, folded and bagged it, loaded it on our wagons or sleds and took it to the train for dad to deliver. We all had to work as the family had so little money.

We also had our jobs in the summer. We had our gardens to tend. We weeded, picked, and prepared for canning. We picked wild berries and helped can them too. Dad would watch for the blueberries to ripen, and then pitch our tent on the river bank. He'd give us a pail for picking. We'd have a lunch break and then get back to picking. At the end of the day, we'd go back to camp and swim and play until dinner was ready. My dad and brother would clean and box the berries for shipping to the larger cities. We were paid by the box.

When we were older dad had more lumber camps in the little towns around us. He would stay at the camps a few days at a time. In the summer he would take us with him, drop us off at the park at Round Lake, pitch the tent, give us a box of groceries, and tell us that he'd pick us up on his way back in a few days. He really trusted us.

He was teaching me to drive in town on our gravel roads one day when he said: "Why don't you ask your mother if you can go with me tomorrow as I will be coming home in the afternoon and will be driving on the country roads. You can do the driving for me." Morn gave the okay and I was so excited.

Driving the two lanes was fine but soon we turned onto the dirt trails heading for the woods. Wouldn't you know it? Another car came towards me. We had to share the road. I didn't move over enough, causing us to scrape fenders. We stopped and found my fender had a dent. Dad said: "Don't worry, next time you will judge it better. We will stop by Surrell's garage. He'll fix it before we go home and your mother won't even notice it. It will be our little secret." A week later I passed my driver's test.

STORY FIVE

My First Paid Job

Blaney Park Resort is a resort where one could relax and be catered to, play golf, tennis, and do all kinds of activities. My two older sisters both had worked at the famous resort before and now it was my tum. My sister Viva, who was two years older than me, decided to go to Grand Rapids to go to a business college and skip working at Blaney for the summer. My sister Ella, who was six years older, had worked there the year before and was going back to be a head waitress another summer. I had just graduated from high school so I decided to apply too. She told me that they wanted people that could smile easily and be very happy with the guests. I really was scared to apply as this was a "real job" and this was my first. I don't think I wiped the smile off my face all summer, as I did get a job in the dining room as a "bun and relish" girl. In the morning at breakfast I wore a bun warmer which was like a metal box that I carried in front of my waist with a strap around my neck and a cover that I opened. The guest could choose their sweet roll or bun at lunch or dinner. I fixed a relish tray that I offered to each person.

After breakfast I was given the menu for the lunch and dinner and I would run them off on a little copy machine. It had carbon paper on a roller that you would crank to make the new menu.

I would have free time between lunch and dinner and again after dinner. We could use all the facilities as long as we stayed out of the guests' way. I learned so many sports. We could use their pool day or night. I dated the golf pro so I really learned the game and the same with horseback riding. He taught me to ride English style where you would hold the reins in front of you, hands close together and stand on your stirrups with a stand and sit rhythm. I usually rode Western where you held your reins in one hand and the other on the front of the saddle. Tennis courts were available for tennis and sometimes we would roller skate on the court.

In the evenings they would have dances in the dining room with Ivan Kabosic's Orchestra or they would have a barbecue dinner on the lake shore. I worked about four summers and a couple of winters when the hunters would come during deer season. We lived in a huge dormitory over the dining room of the inn. Sometimes I would wait on tables and other times I would be head waitress or the cashier. I really enjoyed working there. My sisters and I went back to two reunions since then. The big Celebeth Hotel and the Tnn where the dining room was were the only buildings open. Everything else was closed. The Celebeth Hotel had been remodeled for a bed and breakfast and the fnn or dining room was being rented out for weddings, dances and reunions. It brought back so many fun memories. It was hard to see the changes. It was a ghost town.

STORY SIX

School Days

I graduated from Newberry High School in June of 1939.
I really had a wonderful time. We were a group of boys and girls
that hung around together. Most of us grew up together so we
knew each other pretty well. We all seemed to like the same
activities. In the summer we would roller skate either on the
sidewalks or in the roller rink. We swam in the lakes that were
near Twin Lakes, which was an old gravel quarry four or five
miles from home. Manistique Lake and Round Lake were about
30 miles away where we could pitch our tents and spend our
summer vacations there. We had lots of school dances. Also
our families took us to the dances at the Grange Hall. As we got
older in high school we were allowed to go to Brown's Tavern.
None of us drank in those days. Our bowling alley was open year
around so we bowled a lot. We also played tennis. In the winter
we ice skated-sometimes on the hard, snow-packed sidewalks
or at the ice rinks, frozen rivers, or ponds. We weren't allowed on
the bigger lakes unless our parents were with us to check the

depth of the ice, making sure we wouldn't break through thin ice. We also went snow shoeing, skiing, and ski jumping.

One year we built our own ski jumps halfway down the hill (called "Mount Steepy"). We piled logs and branches into a big pile, then covered it with plenty of snow and packed it down hard. We climbed to the top of the hill, put on our skis with our toes tucked well under the one little strap, and down we went over our new ski jump at a real high speed and out into the air, landing 30 to 35 feet below, hoping we didn't fall as we made it to the bottom.

I also played girls basketball and played trumpet in the high school marching band. The band always played during the school football or basketball games through the first half. Then we would put our instruments away, take off our band uniforms, put on our warm clothes and head for the ice rink which was just outside on the football field. The city recreation department :flooded the frozen field several times, getting a frozen sheet of ice for our rink, and brought in a little building with wooden benches for skate changing. It had a pot-bellied stove for warmth. The man in charge sat at the one window and played the record machine for music. He used the bullhorn to call out the names of games we were to play as we skated. Sometimes he would call "couples only" so you could skate with your date or a friend around and around the rink until the music stopped. If he called "three in a group", three people holding hands skated until he called "center person go forward and join the couple ahead," which changed your group completely. He also might say "free skate" or "everyone tum around and skate backwards" or "crack the whip", where everyone held hands in a long line.

The first person stood still, the rest skated forward around and around, the outside went faster and faster until the far end whipped off the circle, possibly landing on his bum.

One day my mother offered to drive me and a couple of my friends to a championship game that was to be played at Sault Ste. Marie, another town a few hours away. After the game we would have dinner before driving home, so everyone should bring some money--enough for a hot roast beef sandwich-which consisted of a slice of bread cut in half on a plate with a slice of beef on each, a scoop of mashed potatoes in the middle, carrots on the side with roast beef gravy covering all. The parents agreed and off we went. The game was great and we won the championship! We also went to the restaurant and had a delicious hot roast beef sandwich. After we finished mother said we could go "window shopping" for one hour as she still had some shopping to do for herself.

None of us had any money but it was fun to look. We went to Montgomery Wards, Sears & Roebuck, JC Penney, Kresgy's and Woolworth's. We covered them all. We got back to the car just as mom did. We started home after a wonderful day. We were half-way home when mom noticed the noise in the back had changed from laughing to giggling. She looked in her rear view mirror and noticed everyone looking at some jewelry. One of the girls said she took it from Kresgy's Dime Store. Mom heard that and pulled the car over to the side of the road and stopped. We had to tell her that we had dared each other to take something without paying for it. We all had something-a pin, a ring, a necklace.

Mom just said, "That's stealing." She turned the car around and took us all the way to Sault Ste. Marie, back to each store. She had us give back the loot and apologize to the head clerk. I was embarrassed and felt very guilty, and yet proud of my mom. It was a quiet trip home. We arrived much later than we planned. When we dropped the other girls home, Mom just said "We were delayed-your daughter will explain." We all learned that stealing wasn't fun. I don't believe that any of us would try that game again.

STORY SEVEN

Switch Decision

When I was around seven years old my mother let me hang out with my older sister Vi, who was nine, and my brother Sterling, who was eleven. We had a few places that we could not go to and one was the sandpit near our park. One day we headed to the park until we saw a group of children going on to the sandpit. It had rained the night before which left a lot of big water puddles in the bottom. It was tempting so my brother said we could go and see what the other children were doing. We soon got involved in taking our shoes off and waded in the water. All of a sudden Vi screamed and yelled. My older brother, who was in charge ofus, ran and found Vi's foot bleeding. She had stepped on a big piece of broken glass. The puddle was turning red. My brother grabbed my hand and pulled me with him up the hill, telling Vi he was going to call Mom from a house. "I'll take Carmie with me!" he shouted. He knew we were in trouble but he also knew he had to call Mom. We were only 10 or 15 blocks from home.

He knocked on the door of the nearest house. A lady came out right away when I told her what had happened. She called my mom and the message got out over the telephone that connected the whole neighborhood. We went back to Vi. One of the older kids had taken Vi's stocking and tied it around the cut to stop the bleeding. Another friend yelled "Your mother is coming now!" She had grabbed the torn old sheets that she had prepared for bandages and the mercurochrome for disinfectant.

When the grocery delivery man saw my mother, he automatically picked her up. My mom rode on the running board with her hair flying in the wind. She ran to Vi and cleaned and bandaged her foot. The delivery man carried Vi up the hill to his truck. They drove to the hospital. Mom was yelling to us to get right home, and said "I will deal with you two when I get home!" We were frightened because we knew we were in big trouble. We also knew we shouldn't have disobeyed. She couldn't get me out so she just left me and Sterling came in with a good big stick. I finally thought I had better come out and get a switch too. I broke off a little tiny thin stick. We both got a whack across our bottoms. I learned to never cut a skinny stick as it stings more than the thick ones. I also learned to never disobey and to never, never hide under the bed. You get it twice as hard when you do come out. Mom knew that Vi had learned her lesson too. They would never do it again. Our switch decision was the pits, and we got the switch!

STORY EIGHT

The Worst Punishment Ever

I was around nine or ten years old when I started spending the summers with my cousins. My Uncle Bernard McTiver was in charge of the state Conservation Department of Fish and Game. The McTivers had a huge three story house for the family of Bernard, his wife Dean, and their children. The attic was the school room for home schooling their four young children-Jean, Shirley, Bob and Carol. A crew of several men worked and lived in the men's camp. Their jobs consisted of fighting fires and keeping equipment ready. They were game wardens and cared for the fish and wild animals, especially during fishing and hunting seasons. The men always had to make fire lanes through the forest which were roughly cleared roads to get through the woods in case of fires. The station also had a water tower for spotting fires. One person had to climb the ladder to the top of the tower where there was a small room with windows on each side.

He would look through his binoculars over the treetops and if he spotted smoke or fire the phone alarm would be rung with codes for other towers. The rings would be one short and two long or two short and one long. The water towers would sound the alarm and send directions to all other stations. There were several other stations all over the Upper Peninsula of Michigan. Each station was on or near a lake in case of needing more water. Our station was near Perch Lake and our ring was one long and two short.

We kids loved to climb the ladder and visit with the man on duty. Bernard would take us with him when he had to go to another station. We would ride in the back of his truck. We knew all of the other families and liked to play with their kids. We'd swim, catch polliwogs, climb their tower, or anything else we could think of.

When we were home we usually had chores to do in the morning like setting the table, doing the dishes, feeding the chickens, and taking the cows out of the barn. We would hang out the wash one day and do the ironing the following day with heating the irons on the stove. We also had to tend the garden with planting, weeding, and picking. Then we would can the food. When we finished our chores we were free to go play until dinner time.

One day someone showed us how to make magic appear right in front of your eyes. You wrote your name on your hand with soap, and then you burned paper to make ashes. You'd rub the ashes on your hand and your name would magically appear.

We had to try it ourselves. Jean ran to the outhouse to get paper from the Sears catalog. Bob went to the men's camp for wooden matches, and I took the soap from the kitchen sink. We gathered together under the back porch to practice our magic. It worked pretty well until we ran out of paper. We decided to go down the fire lane to the Old Headquarter Creek where we knew the beavers were building a darn. We pulled sticks out of the dam and watched the water flow out. We made a wigwam with the sticks we pulled out.

We had our lunch, waded in the creek, and then we were bored. We thought of the magic again and remembered we still had the soap and matches. I looked around and spied the dry pine needles in the fire lane. They were dry so they should bum and make ashes. We scrambled around the fire lane and gathered the dry pine needles. Bob gave each of us some wooden matches and we built our own little fires like the Indians do. We took turns with the soap and wrote our best friend's name on the back of our hands. It worked-we thought we were the best!

It was getting late so we decided we better get home, but first we had to make sure that the fires were out. We collected green pine needles and put them on our dead ashes. We knew that green wood wouldn't bum. We stamped on them a little and went home.

Our dinner was ready so we washed our hands and sat at the table. While we were eating we suddenly heard a banging on our door. Uncle Bernard answered the door saying, "What's the matter?" A man yelled, "We think we have a fire quite close to here!" We all jumped up.

He said he had the truck out in front with the water cans and was heading down the fire lane. "Coming with us?" Bernard ran out and jumped on the truck. They were heading down our fire lane. We ran out and took a shortcut through the woods. We saw a huge fire. Bernard saw us and told us to get out of there and go home. He and the others were putting the fire out, and we saw him checking our footprints on the fire lane. I knew we were in BIG trouble. We ran home and ran upstairs to bed.

We didn't get up early in the morning until my uncle had gone to work. No one said anything to us. I was afraid because I overheard him telling his wife Dean that it was quite a big fire but that they were able to contain it quickly. The fire was never mentioned to me until years later when I was coming home from college and my train stopped at a little town called Engadine. It was several miles from my home so Dad asked Uncle Bernard, who was in the area, if he would pick me up. The train was on time and Uncle Bernard was on time. I was frightened as I remembered the forest fire we had started. Thoughts were in my head. I'd felt guilty for years. Would he talk to me now, or had he forgotten it?

He put my luggage in the truck. It was very quiet for a few miles. Then Uncle Bernard asked me if I remembered the fire near his house when I was a child. At last he was talking about it. "Yes, I do remember, and I've felt guilty all these years. That was the worst punishment I've ever had. Please forgive me," I said. I still expected to be in trouble until I saw a half-grin on his face. He then smiled and said "Of course you are still a part of our family and you can always visit with us anytime you want to."

STORY NINE

Easter Sunday at Roeding Park

The children could hardly wait. We had already gone to church and had celebrated the Resurrection of Jesus Christ. We also watched all of the ladies and girls dressed in their best with their beautiful hats to parade around in. The men and boys wore their ties. It was a wonderful day already. Before church we had checked our nests that we had made the night before. We had colored eggs and then made our individual nests out of our clothes which we twisted and folded, forming them into nests for the Easter bunny to find and fill with goodies. Sure enough, the nests were filled with eggs with candy inside.

Ken and I promised the kids a day at the park. The City of Fresno Recreation Department and John Muir grade school were having an Easter egg hunt by the cement slab at Roeding Park. It would start at 2:00 sharp. We were to gather at the rope at the top of the hill. No one was allowed on the other side of the rope until the whistle blew and the hunt began.

It would be followed with school dances and square dancing on the slab. We arrived at the park early so dad stopped near the old train that we could climb all over and play as much as we wanted. We still had time to ride on the other train that circled the park. We finally found the slab and a picnic table close by. We were hungry and ready for lunch which consisted of deviled egg sandwiches, a thermos jug of beans, hard boiled eggs that were colored the night before and some cool lemonade. We would have candy for dessert after we filled our baskets.

It was time for the Easter egg hunt. Jim had found some of his friends and off he went to the rope. Deby took Kathy's hand and went to the rope, where they eagerly waited for the whistle. It blew-what fun-all the children scrambled down the hill shouting "here's one, there's one, look in the bushes", filling their sacks, bags, pockets and baskets. They arrived at the slab ready to dance. The little ones hung on to their parents' hands. The bigger children found their friends, teachers, or recreation coaches. Then the children's square dances began. At the end the parents joined in for more square dancing. The slab was full. The whole family had fun. The end came too soon. Everyone was so happy. While dad packed the car the kids and I put on our roller skates for one more turn around the cement slab before going home, tired but happy and full of candy eggs.

STORY TEN

The Titanic

We hear so much on television today of the 100th anniversary of the sinking of the Titanic. The horrible tragic story tells of the first beautiful luxury ship that sank and killed so many people in 1912. I was about 11 years old when I first heard about it. We were sitting around our pot-bellied stove in our living room, trying to keep warm. Dad usually had a story to tell us before bedtime. It seems that it was the 20th anniversary of the sinking of the Titanic. Everyone was again talking about it. My brother was bringing in the firewood from the wood shed. My oldest sister was checking the "hot" baked potatoes from the oven, getting them wrapped in flour sack cloth to tuck in our flannel sheets at the foot of our beds to warm our feet when we went to bed. In the morning the potatoes would be peeled and chopped with the Calumet baking powder can, put in a fry pan with bacon grease from another can and fried for breakfast. The story of the Titanic struck a chord in our hearts-a family memory I'll never forget.

Now I am remembering the movie "Titanic" which came here to Fresno. Everyone was talking again and we all wanted to see it, including Kathy's friend, Julie, and her mother, Maria.
I wondered if the long hours would be too much for Kathy and Julie but thought we would give it a try. We took two cars and went early so we wouldn't have to stand in line. I saw Maria pull into a parking stall and I hurriedly did the same. Kathy and I jumped out of our car to catch up with them. The line for tickets was long but we made it. We had to get popcorn and cold drinks. Again, we managed and finally found our seats. The movie came on and we really enjoyed watching it. I reminisced about all of the old 1900's furniture, dining halls, chandeliers, and clothing-all once so beautiful and now heading to the bottom of the ocean.

The movie was finally over and it was time to leave. We had been talking to everyone in the lobby. We were there for about 2 ½ hours.I started to get my car keys out of my purse as it was now getting dark outside and my car was way out in the parking lot by the fence. I couldn't find my keys. We went back in the movie theater, looked under our seats, checked the restroom, asked the ticket office, but they hadn't been turned in. What to do next? We started to walk towards our cars and decided that Maria would drive us to our house to get my second set of keys and then come back for my car. By then we were near our cars. I looked at mine and the door on my side was open. As I got closer, I heard a noise. My motor was running. My keys were doing their job. Luckily I still had enough gas to get home.

My memories of the Titanic I will never forget, but the memories of my car no one will ever let me forget!

STORY ELEVEN

The Color Purple

After leaving the Ice Capades Ice Show my husband Ken and his partner, Ed Raiche, decided to build a gym here in Fresno called the M & R Health Club. It was in downtown Fresno across from the post office. We were already teaching swimming and coaching diving and weightlifting. Ken and Ed were asked to go back to the Ice Capades for a couple more years, so they hired Harold Zinkin to run the health club for us and we finally sold it to him. When we came back to Fresno, Ken managed the Hacienda Hotel. Our family grew and we loved Fresno. Our children Jim, Deby and Kathy swam and played at the Hacienda pool, the Mermaid pool, and at the Wildwood Country Club.

I became aware of Special Olympics when my daughter Kathy, who has Down Syndrome, was eight years old. Eunice Kennedy Shriver had started the program a couple of years before. She thought that individuals with special needs, like her sister, needed something special that they could excel in and feel good about too.

They started out with two sports-track and field and swimming. We had already taught Kathy to swim. We decided to try it.

Deby and Jim were in school and Kathy was going to the Fresno County Schools' Special Education program. Deby got some of her friends from school to help. We got some of Kathy's school friends and would pile into our Volvo and head to the Frank H. Ball Park pool. We didn't need seat belts in those days and nobody counted heads. I started my new job and favorite hobby of coaching Special Olympics. Kathy already loved swimming and swam all strokes, especially the butterfly.

She started winning the gold in the local Special Olympics competition, went on to the state, national and international levels. New Special Olympics sports were added and gymnastics was next. Again Kathy excelled. Her sister was a gymnast and competing in Nationals and Kathy imitated her. My family and I went on to coaching gymnastics, roller skating, soccer, ice skating, tennis, softball, weightlifting, horseback riding, and bowling.

I had continued to coach or teach ice skating at our ice rink-both figure and speed skating. Our Special Olympians were competing locally and in the southern meet in Los Angeles. We were asked to host the state meet in Fresno, and held it at Icelandia for a few years until we were offered to hold the meet in Selland Arena. We reserved hotel rooms across the street for all of the teams. Several beauty parlors volunteered to do makeup and hair. And the media agreed to be there too.

It was a three day event. We had done our practicing, invited skaters from all over the state. Friday night arrived-their rooms were ready, and our skaters were handing out goodie bags donated from the LARCS and fruit baskets were in the rooms for the skaters, coaches and families.

Early Saturday morning breakfast was served from 6:00 to 8:00 at the hotel. The other event director, Pat Sims, was going to check out everything at Selland Arena, and I was to greet our skaters and families at breakfast at the hotel. I went around visiting everyone, and they were all happy and ready to start. I was so excited and ready for the beginning of a great day.

I then went over to the rink. Everything seemed fine. My partner, Pat, came over, took one look at me, and started to laugh. She said: "What did you do to your eyes? Your eyebrows are purple." My daughter, Deby, came over to see what was so funny. She too burst out laughing. "Oh mom, the media will be here soon." I was to be interviewed, and I had left my makeup at home! The beauticians hadn't arrived and no one seemed to care. They just laughed. I wiped off the purple. My daughter came up with a lead pencil which didn't help. In my hurry to meet everyone in the early hour I had used my purple eyeliner instead of my brown eyebrow pencil. I looked like a clown. No one at breakfast mentioned it but by the time I talked to the media the beauticians had fixed me up.

Things went well after that. We all had a great time. Many medals went home with the skaters. We continued holding the Special Olympics Ice Skating competitions until I retired in 2007 at age 87.

The biggest joy of my life with Special Olympics was that it brought my whole family together for many years as we watched Kathy win state, national and four world titles in gymnastics, ice skating, swimming and rhythmic gymnastics.

STORY 12

Dating

When I was a freshman in high school (1936, Newberry, Michigan), we started forming a group of boys and girls who hung out together. We went ice skating, roller skating, skiing, etc. We began to go to football, hockey and basketball games, and to the movies. We started to have parties in our homes, making fudge or having a taffy pull. Two people would pull it with long ropes and the taffy would end up wrapped around each other. Like most teenagers we'd end up playing spin the bottle and other kissing games. This made us start to "couple up". As time went by we'd be dating one boy for a while and then another one from our group the next week.

By the time I became a senior I usually had a steady boy-friend. He would come to my house and pick me up and take me to the movies, sports, proms, etc. Sometimes we'd trade off and maybe date someone we'd met from another nearby town. If a senior boy had his driver's license and was able to drive his dad's car, he would drive a group of boys to our town's skating rink.

We girls would skate with them and then go out with them to a teen/adult night club to dance.

After I graduated I found a summer job at a summer resort called Blaney Park. I worked as a waitress so I had free time after the meals were served. I dated guys I worked with, plus the young man who was in charge of the horses. He taught me to ride them both Western style and English style. We went horseback riding along Lake Michigan. I also dated the golf pro so I learned how to play golf.

After the summer job was over I went back home to Newberry. I had planned on going to Grand Rapids, Michigan, to a business college. One of my guy friends, Ruben, from Blaney Park had invited me to his home town, Manistique, Michigan, to go to a farewell dance. World War II had just started and a lot of his friends had been drafted to go into the service and would be leaving soon. I had been on my own all summer so my mom just said okay but don't be out too late. Ruben picked me up early and we drove about 60 miles to the dance. Lots of our friends were at the dance. Ruben started drinking beer with his buddies. Most of his high school friends had gotten their draft papers. He didn't want to leave. He only wanted to drink with his friends. It was late! I had to get home! Finally another friend put him in his car and told me to drive us to my home. I hadn't had my driver's license for very long and had little experience driving at night. I was scared! Ruben was singing—he was happy as a lark! I was mad, scared and worried! It was the worst 60 miles of my life. It was very dark, and I had to watch as a deer might be crossing the road. It was very late. I knew my parents would be worried!

It was broad daylight when I arrived home. I parked Ruben, who was sleeping in the back seat of his car, a half block away from my house. I left him there! I didn't want to see him again. My mom was pacing the floor. She looked terrible! She screamed and shouted at me and told me to go to bed. I lay on my bed, crying. She wouldn't listen to me. My dad came in and put his arms around me. I told him how I tried to come home and how I finally had to drive myself. He said: "You must understand why your mom was so worried and she listened for every car to stop. She paced the floor, looked out the window and watched the clock tick. She couldn't go to bed. She kept thinking something terrible had happened to you." Later I was able to go into her bedroom and explain what happened and she understood! I told her I would never get into that kind of predicament again!

A couple of years later Ruben called. He was in the navy and happened to be in Los Angeles, California. He heard I was in the Ice Capades. He wanted to meet me to apologize. I said of course and he came to my hotel. He gave me a jewelry box that he had made especially for me. I still have it! A lesson I remembered for the rest of my life. Have a Plan B to go home!!

STORY THIRTEEN

Special Olympics World Games

Dublin, Ireland, 2003

Pat Sims and her daughter, Ronni, Kathy and I were very excited as we were going to Dublin, Ireland, to see the Special Olympics 2003 World Summer Games. We were planning on leaving Fresno at 5:00 p.m. on June 20, 2003, driving to Millbrae to stay overnight at the El Rancho Motel and leaving the next day from San Francisco for Dublin. We were going to fly via British Airways to Heathrow Airport in London and then transfer to an Aer Lingus flight to Dublin. We would leave Pat's car at the El Rancho Motel until June 30th and pick it up on the way home. Issues with Pat's car prevented us from leaving Fresno until 7:00 p.m., but we got to the motel okay.

Things were going well until we got up in the morning. We were getting dressed and ready for a leisurely breakfast as our plane didn't leave until afternoon. All of a sudden Pat said "my crown's fallen out!" That changed our plans completely. She got out the phone book and found a dentist nearby-Dr. Tsai-who said to come right in. Luckily the dentist was only a mile away, and she fixed the crown, leaving us time to eat and take the shuttle to the airport to catch our plane.

We enjoyed the flight, saw "Chicago" and Star Trek Nemesis", ate a great meal, and landed in London. We then went on to Dublin. At the Dublin Airport, we changed some of our American money to Euros and got our directions for our Bed and Breakfast in Dalkey, Ireland. We found the bus that took us near Dublin's Tara DART station (like the San Francisco BART). There was an escalator to take us up to the platform. Somehow I had mislaid my ticket, but then located it, and started to head up the escalator. We each had two bags. We managed to get on by putting one bag on and then pulling another bag on behind. Pat, Ronni and Kathy made it. My turn came and I put one bag on first, then I stepped on pulling the other bag on behind me. We all were on our way up when all of a sudden the bag behind me fell toward me, clipping me behind my knees, causing me to fall backwards on the bag. I couldn't get my feet under me to get up. I was flat on my back going up feet first. Pat was at the top calling: "Are you alright?" All I could do was laugh. I finally got both my hands on the right side railing and let the forward force of the escalator pull me up. By then Kathy was at the top and Ronni and Pat helped her get off. I finally made it to the top. The DART train was ready to leave. The doors opened, other people threw our bags on for us, we jumped in, and we were introduced to the DART which we used everyday we were there. We got off at Dalkey, a little town south of Dublin. We called Pamela Hughes, the owner of the Bed and Breakfast, who soon came to meet us. She had a tiny car and we had way too much luggage to fit.

She called over a couple of strangers, young men who had a car, and solicited them to help us out. They packed us in and followed her to her house about eight blocks away. We carried our bags upstairs to our rooms. We were supposed to go to the Opening Ceremonies at Croke Park-Pamela told us that we would never make it in time by train, so she offered to drive us there. She dropped us as close as she could, and told us to follow the crowd to the park.

We arrived at the park and we were very hungry as we had not eaten since breakfast except for a few peanuts they gave us on the plane. We had exchanged a small amount of money at the airport, but didn't understand the worth ofEuros. We each ordered a hot dog and hoped we could pay for them. We had enough. Kathy dropped hers, but a man saw her drop it and gave her another. We had great seats down front, and the Opening Ceremonies was spectacular with the big Parade of Athletes of all the countries, especially Team USA, and performances by U2, the Corrs, Riverdance and appearances by Pierce Brosnan and Nelson Mandela. We started exchanging pins and t-shirts, putting the pins on our hats or on a lanyard around our necks. We saw all our Fresno athletes and wished them luck as their competition started the next day. We had a great time and when it was over we followed the crowd out of the stadium. Sure enough we were told that we were heading in the right direction to Connolly DART station. We arrived around 11 :30 p.m. only to hear that the station was closed. They were not open late as everyone thought. The buses didn't run after 10:00 either. Every comer was packed with people waiting for cabs. The city was overcrowded with people form all over the world.

It was dark and scary standing with strangers, not knowing where you are and where you are going, and no phone. It was after midnight when we finally got a cab. We tried to explain where we wanted to go, and finally he did find our home in Dalkey, and accepted our American money. We had a good night's sleep after a long, hectic day.

We had received our packets which explained where the venues were for the different sports. We learned to "follow the crowd" and ride the DART. Our athletes won the gold in gymnastics, rollerskating, and bowling. We also had time to visit lots of castles, pubs, shops and to tour the beautiful city of Dublin.

All good things have to come to an end. Closing Ceremonies was great but sad. The athletes had made a lot of new friends and hated to leave them. We got up at 3 :00 a.m. on the morning of June 30, 2003, and then took a cab at 4:00 a.m. to the Dublin Airport. The weather had been beautiful all week, but it was pouring that morning. The flight to London was delayed for an hour. We finally took off, landed at Heathrow, and decided to stop and change our Euros back to dollars. We were going to go from one terminal to another when we were stopped by the officials who told us that we couldn't proceed because there was a bomb threat. We had to wait for an hour while the terminal was completely checked and cleared. We finally got the clearance, and continued to our gate and found that they had given our seats away! We had to go negotiate a new flight. They were going to send us to Los Angeles, but the car was in San Francisco! Finally we got tickets to San Francisco via Seattle. The plane was smaller, and my friend Pat had been walking on a sprained ankle the entire trip. It was very uncomfortable as the seats were smaller and closer together. We did not get much sleep at all. We made it to Seattle and were so glad to be back on U.S. soil! We started to go through customs to get back into the U.S.A. The others went through quickly but I had to be patted down, take off my shoes and check my purse. They had an escalator straight up to the next floor. I told the others to go ahead and I would catch up when they finished checking me. They finally let me put my shoes back on so I could get on the escalator. I was halfway up when the customs person yelled that I had forgotten my purse. We were really running close to our flight time, and finally I got my purse and we took off as fast as we could to catch our flight with Alaska Airlines. We told Ronni, "Go ahead and tell them we are coming as fast as we can! Tell them to please wait for us!" She did, and they were so gracious to hold the flight for us.

We landed in San Francisco-almost home-and went to get our luggage. Unfortunately it was not there. The kind lady who helped us with our claim for lost luggage greeted us with an Irish accent! We then went on to the motel, got Pat's car, and headed to Fresno. We had hardly slept for two days. Pat drove for as long as she could before she said that she needed to get a little sleep, so we pulled into a parking lot in front of a Target store in San Jose and took a little nap in the car. After about 30 minutes of sleep, we drove through a McDonald's to get some coffee, and continued on our way. We finally made it to Fresno and Pat actually went to work the next day. Our bags took a long time to arrive-more than two weeks. When we finally got the bags they were still damp from the rain.

As hectic as the trip was to and from, we really had fun and if anyone would ask us to do it again, we would do it in a minute. It was quite an adventure!

STORY FOURTEEN

My Skiing Adventure

It was late October 1938 when I was a boyish teenager of 17 in Newberry, Michigan. My friends and I loved to ski. We could hardly wait for the first snowstorm. We didn't care about the weather. We'd put on an extra sweater if it was cold with an extra scarf to wrap around our neck or tie around our face with only our eyes showing. Clear, snowstorm, blizzard or bitter cold, it was all the same. We loved to ski cross country, small hills or to the big hills for ski jumping.

One day after a huge snowstorm the snow was light and fluffy. It would pack down just right for fast downhill skiing. Our skis were family size (one size fits all) with one little strap to hold them on. I'd put a rubber band around my ankles cut from an old tire inner tube. I would put my foot through the strap on the ski and then stretch the rubber band down over my toe. That held the skis securely on my feet, yet it would break easily or come off if I fell. We decided to try skiing that day after school. We had plenty of time to ski before dinner, so we did and had a great time!

One day after a huge snowstorm the snow was light and fluffy. It would pack down just right for fast downhill skiing. Our skis were family size (one size fits all) with one little strap to hold them on. I'd put a rubber band around my ankles cut from an old tire inner tube. I would put my foot through the strap on the ski and then stretch the rubber band down over my toe. That held the skis securely on my feet, yet it would break easily or come off if I fell. We decided to try skiing that day after school. We had plenty of time to ski before dinner, so we did and had a great time!

The next day we were all excited to ski again. The fluffiness had disappeared as it froze during the night leaving an icy crust on the top of the snow. As we skied, the snow would pack down, making it fast and slippery. We decided to go to the hills to do some jumping. We had to ski cross country to get there—through the apple orchards, the woods, and down through the valley. The biggest hill was called "Mount Steepy". The skiers had previously built a ski jump halfway down the hill using old fallen logs and stumps. With the new snow it was just perfect. We had to climb up to the top of the high hill to get enough speed to go down over the jump, out into the air, land and continue to the bottom.

My friend Bob was the first to try. He broke trail, shot off the jump, landed off balance and fell, leaving crusty chunks of frozen snow all over as he rolled and tumbled the rest of the way down to the bottom of the hill. My turn was next. I skied over to the start. I shoved off, dropped down the hill and experienced a beautiful ride. I could see the jump ahead of me. I was going so fast and hit the jump straight.

I shot out into the air, seemed to hover for a moment, landed smoothly, my feet together, but not for long! My left toe on the ski hit a hunk of crusted snow that threw me head first off the trail. I was slipping and sliding so fast on my stomach and face on the icy, crusty snow. My face was scratched from my forehead to my chin. I finally stopped at the bottom. I was finished with my skiing for the day, but stayed and watched the others. We didn't stay long as we had to get home in time to help with dinner and do dishes before going to the high school dance. My mom said that I looked like I had been in a wild cat fight. "You aren't going to the dance looking like that, are you?" "Sure", I answered, until I looked in the mirror and saw the "wild cat that lost the fight" looking back at me.

STORY FIFTEEN

Family Lesson

In September, 1968, I was working at Kelso School with students who have intellectual disabilities, known as "mentally retarded" in those days. One day, I got a telephone call at work from my son, Jim, who was a senior in high school. He usually got out of school around 2:30 p.m. and headed for the kitchen for a snack so I was picturing him eating a sandwich as he proceeded to say, "Mom, you won't be mad at me, will you?" I said, "No Jim, what happened?" He said, "Well, our house is on fire—I got the dog out. I'm at the neighbors' house. Don't worry, the firemen are there." The reality of the conversation sunk in so I said in a "mom controlled voice", "I'll be right home. Call your father!" I was home in 15 minutes and Ken was already there. The firemen were finishing up. Our home was damaged all over. The kitchen, dining room, den and hallway were badly burned with water dripping and puddling everywhere.

Jim had put a pot of grease on the stove to make french fries and forgot about it when he got sidetracked in the garage, starting to prepare for a party in the evening.

He had been playing drums with a neighborhood band and he was hanging blankets on the garage walls to drown out the sound so the neighbors wouldn't complain. He had forgotten the hot grease until he heard it explode. He ran to the kitchen and tried to put the fire out. The cupboard above was in flames which caught the drumstick he was holding in his hand. His hand started to burn so he threw his drumstick which almost hit the dog, Tina, and then caught the sliding door curtains on fire too! He then got scared, grabbed Tina, and ran to the neighbor's house. They called the fire department, and then told Jim to call me and his dad.

The insurance would have paid for us to stay in an apartment or hotel as the bedrooms were full of smoke and water and the kitchen, dining room and den were destroyed. Ken said, "No, that would be too easy. We will stay here and learn a lesson." We cleaned up the water in the room. We put Deby's gymnastics balance beam on the floor in the hallway which we had to walk on to get to and from the bedroom to the kitchen. I had to cook three meals a day for five of us on my electric fry pan. We learned all right. The fire happened in September and we didn't get our new stove until the day before Christmas, December 24, 1968. We enjoyed a great Christmas breakfast and gave thanks to our Lord for the great sacrifice that he made for all mankind. That put everything in perspective and grounded us to the important things in life which aren't things. Our love carried us through and a lessons was learned by everyone.

STORY SIXTEEN

Home to Newberry

In the summer of 1991, my daughter, Kathy, had qualified to compete in gymnastics for Team USA at the International Summer Special Olympics Games held in Minneapolis and St. Paul, Minnesota. Her sister, Deby, was one of the gymnastics coaches and I went as a parent with my friend, Pat Sims, and her daughter Ronni. Kathy won a gold medal and was given the Spirit of Friendship Award from California Special Olympics.

We were so close to Michigan that Deby, Kathy and I decided to go to my home town of Newberry and I would show Deby and Kathy where their roots came from since Deby had never been to Michigan before. We were able to get plane tickets right away and flew to Grand Rapids where my sister Vi and brother-in-law Dick lived. They drove us up to the Upper Peninsula to where my sister Loretta and brother-in-law Reinard Hemkes lived on the Muskallonge Lake, which was near Lake Superior and north of Newberry where I grew up.

The following day was the 4th of July and a day to be celebrated. We all got up early and drove to Newberry to see the old homestead and to watch the parade and fireworks. We set up our chairs on the curb in front of other relatives homes and immediately found lots of old friends to chat with. The parade started with the Veterans marching with their flags. The school bands played their instruments and batons were tossed and twirled. All kinds of floats went by with riders tossing candy to the children. The older kids had their squirt guns to shoot at the fire trucks. When the firemen turned their water hoses on the kids and anyone else on the curb, people scattered and hid behind the bushes and trees. Everyone got wet! The floats were wonderful with creative decorations and themes.

When the parade was over, everyone headed for the open field by the airport where the carnival would be held. The games and races began—they had the egg toss, the gunny sack race and many more, including catching of the greased pig. Earlier tickets had been sold for the main attraction called The Cow Drop. The tickets were sold for $5.00 with a cash prize of $500.00. A huge field had been squared off with white chalk like a big checker board with 4' X 4' squares. A truck brought a cow in and let it off on the field. Deby had purchased two tickets, one for Kathy and another for her. The carnival continued—the girls were in line for homemade ice cream when they heard a loud commotion. Everyone ran toward the field. The cow had finally "done her duty" on square #23. The numbers were checked and sure enough, Kathy had the winning #23. She was called to the stand to become the grand Queen of the Cow Drop, winner of $500.00. No way was she going to share with her sister!!

They did take a picture of the two of them with the cow and the cow drop #23.

It was time to go to a potluck dinner and then the fireworks before going back to Loretta's house. All of us were worn out, stuffed and happy. We stayed for two weeks, visiting the Soo Locks where the water had to be raised or lowered for ships to pass from one great lake to another. We visited the Tahquamenon Falls—both the upper and lower falls. We crossed the nine-mile long bridge over the Straights of Mackinac connecting Lake Michigan and Lake Huron, and also connecting Lower Michigan to Upper Michigan. We took a boat ride over to Mackinac Island where no automobiles have ever been. On the island only horse and buggy and bicycles are allowed. We also saw the old Indian Fort Mackinac which is now a museum. We then went back to Newberry and saw the state prison which was formerly the state hospital for people with disabilities. We went by the saw mills, lumber camps, and the chemical company which used to make pig iron. We saw lighthouses on the shore of Lake Superior and fire towers in the forests. These are all closed now. We also visited the sand dunes along Lake Superior and looked for agates on the rocky shores. It is truly the land of Hiawatha. We all went home with beautiful memories and a "Cow Drop Queen" crown proudly worn by Kathy.

STORY SEVENTEEN

The 4th of July

We usually spent the 4th of July at Wildwood Beach Club when our children were growing up. It was located just a few miles north on highway 41 on the San Joaquin River. They had a small four-hole golf course, a volleyball court, a huge swimming pool and the river to play in. They also had a huge cement dance floor with a stage and ping pong tables. The picnic tables and barbecue pits were along the river and under the trees. We carried our own lounges or chairs in and out each day—also cribs and playpens. We carried all personal stuff, including food and drink, in and out each day as well. The owners had a little "check in store" with snacks, loudspeaker, changing room with bathrooms and a telephone. We paid our family membership for the summer. We could take a friend but had to pay for them each day.

There was something for everyone in the family to do. We would pick our spot, set up camp for the day (usually the same spot) and scatter. Our kids found new friends and so did the adults. The river curved around, forming an island.

We adults (and some of the kids) would carry our plastic rafts and walk across the river, then walk across the island, enter the river upstream and float back around the island to the club which took about an hour. We could watch the fish or even a snake as we lazily floated with the current. We knew our children were having fun as we all knew the other families and could be called on the loudspeaker if we were needed.

On the 4th of July, they had all kinds of races scheduled at the pool and diving board, and at the end of the day before Sundays or holidays the pool was emptied for cleaning. They would throw a handful of change in the pool for the kids to dive in for. On the 4th of July we would then put all our stuff in our cars before it got dark to be ready to sit on the hillside on our blankets and wait for the fireworks to be shown across the river. The staff would take up a collection of money during the day and buy fireworks and then set them off in the evening on the island. They really did a great job.

On one 4th of July, the staff seemed to work really hard at getting ready for the evening fireworks. They were tying a rope in the trees form one side of the river to the other. It was like a zip line. They each carried an empty basket on their afternoon practice runs. It was to be a grand entrance to their fireworks show. At last it was dark and time to start. Greg went across with fireworks in his basket and sparklers sparkling. He got almost to the other side when Tom, in his anxiety, got on the zip line too soon with the rest of the fireworks. The double weight stretched the rope down, pulling Greg, Tom and all the fireworks into the river. The show was floating downstream.

It was the shortest fireworks performance ever—but everyone had a good belly laugh and it was a night to remember at Wildwood.

STORY EIGHTEEN

Life Changing Holiday

I had been skating with the Ice Capades Ice Skating Show for five years, and felt it was time to leave the show when we got to Chicago. I had auditioned there and it was close to my home where I could try something else. I approached my boss and he asked me if I would consider staying a couple of months longer until they finished this year's show in Los Angeles. Then he would pay my train fare home from L.A. He told me the cast would be taking a two week holiday, and would then rejoin the Capades in Atlantic City, New Jersey, to rehearse the 1946 show. I decided to stay.

World War II was over and some of the fellows were rejoining the Capades. One of them was Ken Mullen, who skated an acrobatic act with his brother Len and Ed Raiche called the "Hub Trio". They had skated with the show before they were drafted into the navy.

I dated Ken for a couple of months and we had a great time together. It was almost time for me to leave. We were walking down the boardwalk in Santa Monica and Ken was begging me to stay on with the Capades. I told him: "No, not with the same name." There just happened to be a jewelry store nearby. He looked at me—then turned me into the store. I thought he was kidding, but we started to look at wedding rings. Sure enough, we found one my size and we decided to buy it. He then said: "It's time for you to talk to our boss and get you rehired."

I did and he said, "Okay, take a two week holiday and then return to Atlantic City for rehearsals." We were so excited and started to make plans right away.

Our train stopped in St. Paul, Minnesota, where my brother was working. We both got off to visit with him, and then transferred to another train go on up north to my home and family, where we would get married. Then we would go on to visit his family in Manchester, New Hampshire, and finally on to Atlantic City. We called my family and they were shocked as they had never heard me mention Ken before and now we wanted to get married. They were happy that we were coming home and said they would make arrangements. We called Ken's mother and she cried as she thought Ken should marry a Catholic girl, which I wasn't. We ran around checking churches and found it would take longer to get married in a Catholic church and decided on a Protestant one. Then we needed a license—by then it was almost 5:00 and all offices were closed. We were told that you had to wait two days after getting a license to get married.

We were so disappointed! My brother had a car so we decided to drive all night and still try to get married the next day in Newberry. My family came through for us. They got our license, the two-day rule was waived and we were married in a Protestant church with most of my family, relatives, and friends attending. They had a reception for us at a summer resort and had rented a cabin for our honeymoon on Halfway Lake.

We had to row a boat across the lake to get to our cabin. We were really in the north woods now. Ken carried me over the threshold and we were finally by ourselves. Ken built a fire in the pot-bellied stove and we immediately had smoke all over the inside of the cabin. The family jokesters had put a pail over the chimney! Ken climbed up on the roof and removed the pail. We found our bedding was soaked—they had dunked them in the lake. We found dry ones in the closet and soon had things livable.

We woke up early in the morning with a horrible noise under our bed. We found a coffee can tied to the springs with a notched spool of fishing line strung through a hole in the can, through a knot-hole in the wall and out into the woods where any wild chipmunk, rabbit, woodchuck, bear or deer could run into it causing the spool to unwind and run around in the can. What a night! We did have a few days to get to know each other with visiting and reminiscing before leaving for Manchester, New Hampshire to meet with Ken's family.

They were so happy to see us and wanted to hear about the wedding. They were glad to hear we were married in a church.

They too rented a cabin for us in the White Mountains on Lake Winnipesaukee. Ken's brothers and sisters planned a family reunion for us—all seven of them, plus their families were there so we did a lot of ball playing, swimming, reminiscing and eating. It was quite late when they all left and we were really tired. We had to leave the next day to go to Atlantic City and back to work.

The cabin had an outhouse down the path and into the woods. It was dark, surrounded with bushes and trees. I started down the path. It was too dark and I was scared. I stepped off the path, squatted in the bushes, and then ran back to the cabin. What a mistake! I woke up with a rash. I could hardly walk. I'm allergic to poison oak or poison ivy. That is what I sat in. Again I had to talk to my boss and tell him I couldn't skate for another two weeks.

So my holiday was extended. Not only was this my longest holiday, but also my most memorable one. It not only changed my name, but in our hurry and excitement, we were married on my birthday, changing it to anniversary. We had 39 wonderful years together.

STORY NINETEEN

Our Surprise Daughter

My daughter, Kathy, who has Down Syndrome, started swimming with her father when she was about five years old. We belonged to the Wildwood Country Club and they had a beautiful outdoor pool which we all loved, especially Ken and Kathy. The city of Fresno is noted for its hot weather so most people have pools in their backyards. Kathy's dad decided she better learn to swim because our neighbors had a pool in their backyard. They did have it fenced in, but they also had five kids and one could leave it open at anytime.

Ken worked with Kathy as much as he could and we then heard that the Kennedy family, via the Joseph P. Kennedy Foundation, was starting a national program for the mentally retarded called Special Olympics. We decided to start a group in swimming too. We found a pool on the west side of Fresno called the Frank H. Ball pool that let us use their pool for teaching.

Deby, who is Kathy's older sister, was going to high school at the time and so she got a group of her friends to help coach. We filled our little Volvo car, which did not have seat belts, with kids and coaches. We worked with any special education kids that parents would bring to the pool every Saturday morning for an hour of instruction. It was free through the Fresno Parks and Recreation Department.

Soon we connected with the local Special Olympics which was created and co-sponsored by the Fresno County Schools Department in 1968. Over the years Special Olympics has brought meaning and a sense of accomplishment to many individuals. They started with track and field and swimming in the beginning, and would have a local meet each spring. The kids were then separated as TMR (Trainable Mentally Retarded) and EMR (Educable Mentally Retarded). In 1970, Kathy won a ribbon at our local meet in swimming and was invited to go to Long Beach, California, for the California State Special Olympics and compete with the eight and nine-year-olds. We didn't know what to expect.

We finally arrived and looked at the big pool. It was completely fenced in. It was the hardest thing I had to do. I had to hand my little Kathy over to a strange woman who took her inside the fenced pool. They did have a coach in the water with her. She had to swim with bigger girls and stay in her lane. When her turn came, she swam beautifully and then looked exhausted. She just seemed to roll as she stroked her freestyle. She still had quite a ways to go. I wanted to take her out! I was thinking "what did I do to this babe?" The fence was too high. It was finally over and she had won the 25 freestyle. She just said "I did it! I did it!"

She had the biggest smile on her face. I thought she was finished but to our surprise she was also scheduled for the 50 freestyle. She was now saying "down and back, down and back!" How could I say no? We did it all over, only it was twice as long. She won that race too. We then found out that today was just a qualifier, and the finals were to take place the next day. She ended up winning the finals too, and received a silver medal in the 50 freestyle and a gold medal in the 25 freestyle—Kathy's first California State Special Olympics title.

Kathy participated in many more sports over the years, and whatever she participated in—she had to win a medal. Kathy is a four-time Special Olympics International champion— in swimming, gymnastics, ice skating and rhythmic gymnastics. She has earned hundreds of ribbons and medals over her 44 year career.

STORY TWENTY

Our Favorite Neighbors

The Nichols family, our neighbors, lived down the street from us in Newberry, Michigan. Bill (Mr. Nichols), was a short, roly poly man who worked at the depot directing all of the trains that came in and out of our little town. His wife, Mrs. Nichols, was a tall, bulky, happy Swedish woman who loved to cook and bake for her family and anyone else who came into her house. They had a large family consisting of ten girls and one boy. The three older girls, LaVern, Margaret and Catherine, were going to college. The next three, Ethel, Vyla and Marion, were in high school. Grace, Helen and Betty were in junior high, and Billy, their one boy, was in grade school. Sally was a toddler and still at home.

Their house was huge—four bedrooms upstairs plus bath and two bedrooms downstairs. There were two empty lots on the other side of their house which we called "Nichols Field." We played baseball and touch football in the summer and in the winter, we rolled snow balls, made forts and battled with the snow balls.

 In the summer the Nichols had a huge garden where we could snack on radishes, carrots and cucumbers whenever we wanted. There were huge apple trees in their backyard with fruit for the picking, and trees in the front where we could climb and carve our initials in the branches. They had a small shed in the back-yard that we would throw a ball over to someone on the other side, yelling "antee antee I over." If someone missed and the ball rolled back down, we'd yell "pigtail" and try again. If the ball made it over and someone caught it, we'd run to the other side and try not to get tagged—caught by the ball.

Mrs. Nichols baked six loaves of bread every other day for her family and one extra for whoever else was there. She loved company. She would break off pieces of that hot bread for all of us to try. It was too hot to cut with a knife. Then she would show us where the homemade apple butter was, saying help yourself. One day she baked a huge coconut cream cake for one of the girls' birthday parties. The party was going to be held in the basement of the church that evening. We were invited and it was time to go. She put on her coat, picked up the huge beautiful cake, took one step and stepped on a toy that made her fly in the air and fall. She ended up sitting under the dining room table, surrounded by pieces of coconut cake. She looked like she was going to cry—then she broke out in uncontrollable laughter, saying "ice cream will have to do!"

Every Sunday morning after Sunday school, we'd go to the Nichols' house to read the funnies in the newspaper. Mr. Nichols would be sitting in his big chair, reading the newspaper and smoking his big cigar.

He would hand us kids the funnies and we would spread them all over the floor at his feet and quietly enjoy them. He loved his kids and us too. We always were welcome at their house and always had lots of kids to play with. Gracie was my sister Viva's best friend and Helen and Betty were mine.

STORY TWENTY-ONE

My Sister Vi

Oh how I miss you Vi. If I could only talk to you! You always had the answers whether it was a name I needed or a memory or just chatter. We could talk for hours at a time—half the night or all day. We've always been like that. You and I were only two years apart. Our job or chores were to do the dishes together and clean the bathroom. We had a lot of the same friends and lived in a small town.

The Nichols family lived down the block. They had eleven kids. You could still rattle off all of their names, starting with the oldest Grace who was your age and Betty was mine with Helen in between. If Betty was invited to stay with me overnight then you had to take her place at her house as Mr. Nichols counted heads every night before he went to bed. If I had an invitation to go out at night and you weren't invited, you had me wash the dishes and you dried. When you dried a dish, you'd sneak it back with the dirty ones and I'd end up washing them over and over, making my friends wait and wait for me to finish.

Or you would have to go upstairs to the bathroom, saying, "I bet you can't finish the dishes before I get back." I was gullible and fell for that for a long time. We would sing our lungs out as we did those dishes—even during family reunions and visits when we were older.

Do you remember when we would go to Junior League at church on Sunday evening? We would pass Mrs. Hunter, our teacher, on the sidewalk and check to see if she was carrying a bag of candy. If she did we would go to class. We always started out singing hymns and you would sing off key and loud on purpose to make the kids laugh. You were terrible! We had to memorize a verse in the Bible and you always said the shortest "Jesus Wept." If I sing at home now, Kathy will say, "that's you and Vi."

We would go to Round Lake and camp in our tents. We had our special call: e-o-o-peep-peep. If you were across the lake in a row boat you would shout e-o-o-peep-peep loud, letting me know where you were and I'd return the call even louder. We still used that call when we would see each other or when we talked on the phone. I miss you so much!

When I graduated from high school, I followed you to Grand Rapids to a business college and moved into Elmcrest, a beautiful home for college students. You had already been there a couple of years. We had a great time together there and then you met Dick Matheson. You really liked him and soon you ran off to the next state and married him. It wasn't the same when you left Elmcrest so I decided to quit college and go back home.

You and Dick asked me to go to Muskegon, Michigan with you to start a new business making and selling red and white cabbage, lettuce, carrots and fresh endive salad in the grocery stores. We had to wash, grind, bag and sell it in the stores. Things were a little rough. You had a little coupe car. My place in your car was on the shelf by the back window all the way to Muskegon where you had rented a one bedroom house where you and Dick slept. I had to climb a ladder to a platform over the bathtub to get into my bed which had a curtain between the bathtub and the toilet for privacy. The business lasted only a few months as the stores didn't always refrigerate the salads at night and we would have to replace the wilted ones. Oh yes, you were pregnant with Sally then too. We all packed up and went back to Grand Rapids.

About that time World War II had started and Dick and I got jobs working in the war factories. Dick soon was drafted in the service. You and Sally moved back home with mom and dad. My job was putting 30 caliber bullets in magazines. I had auditioned with the Ice Capades and got called to join them in Hollywood, California. I only saw you and Dick on vacations, family reunions, etc. Our brother, Sterling, was drafted too. I was so proud and blessed with my three sisters. We were all so close. We got together often in our later years. We all made it to our 90's. It seems like just yesterday that you, Ella, and I got together. We had lost Loretta, but the rest of us had a ball. Then we lost Ella. I was so blessed to be able to talk to you so often. Now I've lost you too. I knew you were ready when I received all your packages. I was so sad to hear you had cancer and you were so ready to get things in order.

I had hoped I could see you in October when my family could take care of Kathy but you and God had other plans. We will see each other again in "His" time.

I love you,

Carmie

STORY TWENTY-TWO

Cheerleading Experience

My daughter, Deby Hergenrader, had taken gymnastics all through her high school years. She did a lot of competing with the schools and the Fresno Gym Club. She won many state, regional and national titles and ended up with the trials for the U.S.A. team. During the competition she injured her ankle and found she could not continue. In her senior year she was still recovering so she turned to diving and cheerleading. When they had their cheerleading competition at camp in Squaw Valley her squad from McLane High School in Fresno, California, won the Pepsi Cola title. Deby also won the top cheerleader award and was hired as a National Cheerleading Association instructor and received a scholarship to attend Fresno State College. She traveled for two summers instructing at several camps in the U.S. and Canada. It was her first job, other than gymnastics.

Her first camp was in Logan, Utah. She was to fly to Salt Lake City and then to Logan, Utah. She had flown before but with a team or a group of girls and coaches.

This time she was by herself and she'd be staying in the dorm at the college. She always called me when she got in. This time she was quite late in calling. Finally I got her call. She seemed out of breath. She said two college boys called her name at the airport and told her they were to take her to the college, so she went with them to pick up her bags and put them in their car. She got in with them. She said they laughed and kidded with her and then she noticed they passed the college and drove on to a wooded area. It was getting dark. They started to whisper and giggle to each other then stopped the car and told her to get out. They pushed her down. Then all of a sudden she said "Mom, I gotta go. I'll call you back." She hung up! I wanted to call her back but I had no number. I had to wait and wait. She finally called. "Deby, what happened?" "Mom, after they pushed me down, they started top pull my leg—just like I'm pulling yours!" There was a pause and then she said—"gotcha, pay back time!" Dad said with a grin—"takes after her mom and dad!!" It took me awhile before I laughed.

STORY TWENTY-THREE

Our Big Red Parachute

A friend of Ken's gave him a big red parachute. We wondered what we would do with it. My son Jim thought it was great. He stretched it out in the backyard, ran down the block, found his friends Betty, Ray and "Money Bags" Glen, and brought them back to show them his new toy. We all got into the fun. We found that if we all grabbed an edge we could pull back and the center would rise in the air, pulling us in towards the center, and then if we pulled back it would come back down. We could circle around with it and flip it up and down, bouncing a ball to each other. It was lots of fun. Jim took it to school for "show and tell" and his class played with it during recess. Like anything else, they soon got tired of playing with it so we put it away upstairs in the garage.

We had a huge apricot tree in our backyard by our patio. It was our favorite tree. It had a nice strong branch for a rope swing.

It also was a good climbing tree with branches close enough to the patio roof that Jim and his friends could climb up the tree, out onto the roof, and up into the window of Jim's upstairs bedroom. It was their short cut. Then the apricot tree became loaded with fruit. The apricots seemed to all ripen at once and started to fall to the ground where they would break open and be useless. Someone thought of the parachute and ran to the garage and brought it back. Dad tied one side on the fence and another on the pole on the patio. The rest was held by Jim and the neighbor kids. They held it waist high. Then Dad got the clothesline prop and would reach up and lift and shake the branches. The apricots would fall onto the parachute without even a bruise. We ate as many as we could and we filled boxes of cots for Mom to can or make jelly with and filled more boxes for the neighbors. The kids played with the chute for awhile and then put it away in the garage again.

Later in the summer Dad Ken came home from work one night and said "I'm taking a few days off so pack the blankets and fry pan, we're going up to the lake." We didn't have a tent. We usually just laid the blankets out on the ground near the lake and slept under the stars in the public park. They always had little iron stoves big enough for a coffee pot and a fry pan. This time Dad brought the red parachute with us too. I was pregnant with Deby at the time so maybe Dad thought we needed more privacy as my brother Sterling was with us too. We were driving an old 1940 Ford station wagon so they tied the parachute to the front headlights, draped it over and around the sides and to the back of the station wagon. It was long enough to extend out over the back, forming a porch at the back.

We staked it out to two clothesline poles. Jim, who was five, and I slept in the station wagon and Sterling and Ken were on army cots in the porch extension of the parachute.

That red parachute became our family tent. As the children grew it turned into many different shapes—we had neighbor sleep-outs in our backyard quite often. Sometimes it was just a lean-to on the side of the garage. Other times it was draped over the clothesline. As our family grew the parachute was used more and more and became tattered and torn and showed its age. We loved that Big Red Parachute. We miss it now but will always have wonderful memories of our travels together.

STORY TWENTY-FOUR

Our London Trip

While traveling with the Ice Capades Ice Show, Ken and I were called into Mr. Harris' office (the owner of the show). Ken's partners, Ed Raiche and Ken's brother Lenny and their wives Voline and Elinore, were already there. Mr. Harris told us that his second show, the Ice Cycles, were going to London, England, from June 22 – September 17, 1949. He wondered if we wanted to go, as they needed a strong act to perform with them. We could catch up with the Ice Capades later in the season. The Ice Cycles was a repeat of the Ice Capades, a year later but playing different cities, using the same show in 1949. We decided to go with them for the short time. We left New York on the Marine Shark, a converted liberty ship taking its last voyage. It was great passing the Statue of Liberty and waving goodbye to so many people in New York.

We went to our rooms, which were like a huge dormitory with individual rooms but all girls on one side and all men on the other. It didn't take us long to trade places so couples could be together.

We strung a lot of sheets across the room to make it more private. It took us nine days to cross the ocean. We would go to the dining room for dinner and when the ocean was rough and made the ship roll, all the other kids would roll with it, making those that got sick sicker.

We finally sailed into London and found we were booked in the Rose Court Hotel. The rooms were very nice but we (all 60 girls) were all on one floor with only one bathroom at the end of the hall. We wanted to get settled some place else soon as we had a few days off and wanted to go to Paris. Someone at the hotel told us where an apartment was available so we took our luggage over there, checked in and took off for Paris. We saw a couple of good shows at a nightclub, the Eiffel Tower, the Arc de Triomphe and walked along the Seine River. We returned to London and found they had rented out our room to someone else while we were gone to Paris. What a mess! We also found we were by the famous wall where the prostitutes hang out. Again we moved to another place called a "dig" which seemed much better but our food that we brought with us because food was still rationed from World War II was disappearing from our trunks. We also would have one sheet changed every fortnight, which was every two weeks. We finally move into a beautiful part of town. We had a very nice, clean furnished apartment with other couples from our group and we had a great time from then on.

On opening night Prince George was attending the show and one of our comedians sat on his lap during his act. The government people converged on them immediately and the comedian was in big trouble.

Pictures were in the newspapers the next day. It did get straightened out so it was okay. We did have a wonderful time and saw the famous ballet dancers. Ken had his American camera with him and he pretended he was a newsman from the U.S. He was able to go in to the palace and take close-up pictures of the Changing of the Guard and the Queen in her carriage.

Ken and I had to fly home early because my father was sick with cancer. I was able to spend a little bit of time with him before he passed away. Then we rejoined the show and finished out the season. It was a time in my life that I'll never forget.

STORY TWENTY-FIVE

Wildwood Country Club 1960-1980

What a wonderful place for us to be when our children were growing up. I think Jim (The Drummer) was around 12 years old and Deb (The Gymnast) was 7 and Kathy (The future 4 Time World Special Olympics Champion and the Inspiration for Break the Barriers) was 2. Kathy was still crawling around in her play pen and just beginning to walk. Wildwood was a Country Club on the San Joaquin River just North of Fresno on Hwy 41. It was a close get-a-way for Moms and Dads, Doctors, Fireman, Carpenters, Plumbers, Laborers, Teachers, etc. - families who liked the outdoors but didn't want to drive very far to enjoy it. Wildwood had a big swimming pool, a small baby pool, a small golf course, tennis courts, sand volley ball courts, horseshoe pits, ping pong tables, and plenty of BBQ's and picnic tables for picnics. AND the river! We would carry our air mattresses across the island, walk upstream then float down around the island to our picnic tables. We would float over small rapids and then over calm water where we would watch the muskrats, beavers, snakes and fish.

On many of the weekends there would be big corporate parties, end of the year parties and reunions in the big picnic area at the end of the park. Many times the Wildwood parents would find out that their kids already ate dinner or lunch with these businesses. Our kids would blend into their food lines and would eat really well because no one knew whether they were a part of their party or not. AND if the party did know they didn't mind sharing because their kids were probably playing with ours.

When Deby and Steve got married they had their wedding reception out at Wildwood. Over 500 people were invited and more people who were not invited saw a party going on from Hwy 41 and decided to join in. Deb and Steve were congratulated by many people that they knew.

Wildwood will always be in the hearts of the families that were blessed to spend many summers there by the river. Each summer was like a family reunion.' We miss it deeply! There has never been another place like it.

STORY TWENTY-SIX

Recognition Dinner

I was never more proud as I was when I went to a Down syndrome yearly dinner on October 24, 2008. I had gone to many such dinners in the past as I have a daughter with Down syndrome and I had volunteered to be on their first board. I knew they were going to honor Marian Karian, founder of Exceptional Parents Unlimited, who I've known for many years. They were also honoring the Educator of the Year, Karen West, who I also worked with while employed with the Fresno County Office of Education. Another volunteer was to be honored too but they didn't say who. Denise Allshouse began the meeting with: "Please join us while we take time to honor individuals in our community who have made a significant difference in the lives of people affected by Down syndrome. It is important to mention people who got us where we are today, pioneers without whom no Down syndrome community would exist. Pioneers are defined as inventors or innovators—a person that is the first to do something or that leads in developing something.

I want to spend a moment to recognize a pioneer right here in our audience tonight." Denise kept talking and she said "she was the first to do" this or that. The more I listened to her, it sounded like my past, bringing up our daughter, Kathy. I didn't think I had done anything special. I just wanted to help my daughter to develop and learn as all other parents do. I will never forget all the good words I listened to that evening. Denise ended with: "She is the first to be honored as a pioneer for our families who have a loved one with Down syndrome.

She is—Carmie Mullen."

STORY TWENTY-SEVEN

Like Mother, Like Daughter

Our daughter Deby always helped me out when I was in a pinch and needed an extra body to fill in, like when our special education school was putting on a Christmas pageant and a student didn't show up on the big day. She automatically filled in the student's spot. She also helped us with our church pageant. She agreed to sign for the Christmas carols in the program, but when none of the two angels showed up she didn't mind wearing one of the angel costumes, and I wore the other, and she signed for the carols too.

One time she and some older girls from the Fresno Gym Club went over to a school on the coast where their coach was teaching gymnastics for the summer. They drove over to help demonstrate for the students. On the way home the girls decided to stop at a pizza parlor in San Luis Obispo which had a dance floor where a group of young men were just waiting for some young girls to dance with them.

The other girls were juniors and seniors and willing, but Deby was only 12 years old. She finally gave in and danced a slow dance with a young man and he held her real close to his body. When she was telling me about it when she got home, she said she was scared as it was the first time she slow-danced with a boy like that and said, "Oh mom, can I get pregnant slow dancing?"

Another day I was making monkey bread in a spring form type angel food pan and I was in the other room when the timer went off. I shouted to Deb to take it out of the oven. She did but when she lifted it out the hot butter leaked through the bottom of the pan, burning a streak of hot butter down her bare legs. She jumped up into the sink and ran cold water over the burns. It helped but I think she still has big scars down her legs.

Another time when she was a young mother she took her four-year-old son, Jared, to K-Mart to shop for skinny jeans. She was in the dressing room and she forced them on but couldn't get them off. Jared pulled and they tried everything in her purse, including putting Vaseline around her ankles, but couldn't get them off. She tried to get Jared to go get a clerk but he wouldn't do it. He was too embarrassed. Finally she shouted as loud as she could and the clerk finally came in. She got some scissors and had to cut them off.

Another time she was shopping with the kids and kept thinking the hem was coming loose from her jeans. As she had taped it with masking tape, she kept reaching down, shoving it back up the pant leg. She got to the cashier and finally stopped and found it was her panty hose that must have stuck in her pants leg when they were washed.

So she pulled the long panty hose out of her pants like a magician pulling a long scarf out of a hat. She told him "these are mine, I promise."

One day she said that her lips were chapped and asked me what to put on them. I was in the other room so I just yelled that there was some salve for chapped lips in the junk drawer in the kitchen. Deb found some and put it on her lips. Immediately her lips started to burn and swelled as big as Al Jolson's. We looked at the salve container and it was for our dog Duke. Deb hadn't read it—she just used it. It was for Duke's itchy crotch. We had to call the poison control center and were told to flush her lips every 15 minutes.

I have done a few dumb things myself—like using bug spray instead of hair spray, making me late for work, or wearing not only one black shoe and one navy shoe, but one flat shoe and one with a small heel, enough to go "clippity clop" down the mall. I wore different earrings, or wore curlers in my hair while shopping. I've told you many of my stories before about setting a forest fire, wearing purple eye brows, etc., etc. These are the things in life that keep us humble.

STORY TWENTY-EIGHT

September, 1945 - Cleveland, Ohio

The Ice Capades is opening in your town. Advance billing has started, billboards are covered. Newspaper campaign has started, radio ads are heard. The trains finally arrive in Cleveland carrying the skaters, staff, and all props and equipment. The staff and the skaters are taken to their hotels in cabs or buses. The props and equipment have been delivered to the ice arena. The trunks and luggage are delivered to the hotels for a two week stay. After checking in and getting settled in our hotel rooms, most of us take a trip to the arena and check out our dressing rooms. We also check the ice to see if it is hard or soft. They use hard ice for hockey games which means if they just had a hockey game we will need really sharp edges on our blades or we will be slipping and sliding on our skates. If so, we better get our skate blades sharpened before opening night. Everything is ready. The ice has been painted so we can judge where we are on the ice when the bright lights are on. The bandstand is over the back-stage area which is all decorated for show time.

We finally arrive for opening night. We use our special entrance door with our I.D. tags, then immediately go to the stage area to check the bulletin board. It will give us any changes of the running order for this evening's show. We will grab our first costume from its wardrobe closet and take it to the dressing room where we will put on our heavier make-up and then our ice skates and finally our beautiful costumes. We will listen for the ten minute call, then the two minute call backstage. The overture starts and we should be lined up on the ice in a blackout at our opening positions. The overture finishes, the lights come on as the music for "Ballet Blue" begins and we move down the ice. The audience explodes with applause as the lights come on showing beautiful, elegant costumes as the skaters seem to float across the ice. Then Champion Bobby Specht and Junior Ladies Champion Donna Atwood appear in an ice operetta called "Toys for Sale" and Bobby has a routine of daring jumps and spins along with Donna with her dazzling stage personality. They wow the audience. The comedian, Eric Waite, Red McCarthy, the speed skater with the painted body who jumped barrels and people, Phil Taylor, a stilt skater and Trixie, the juggler (who I helped by tossing her equipment to her sometimes). Sometimes I'd overthrow a ball and she would run into the audience to retrieve it with her mouth piece. Also included was Joe Jackson Jr. with his collapsing bicycle and Orin Markhus and Irma Thomas, who waltzed to "Shine on, Harvest Moon." These are just a few of the skaters, along with the group numbers, and the acrobats, the Mullen Twins and Ed Raiche, that made the Ice Capades not only the top ranking skating stars but also the greatest collection of talented variety artists ever assembled on ice.

The next day, the Cleveland papers stated that "the ensemble numbers are exceedingly well designed and executed. Much time and talent has gone into these numbers and we cannot speak too enthusiastically of the music, costumes, and general program arrangements, including the vocals and accompaniment. The Ice Capades is the Greatest Show on Ice!"

STORY TWENTY-NINE

The Mirror

Wowwee—the mirror looked back at me so much different than the day before yesterday. Am I sure it's me? I asked all over had I been in a cat fight? Or had I been beaten? Then I remembered—I was in a deep sleep in my comfortable bed the night before when all of a sudden I had great cramps in both of my feet. My feet seemed to twist—there was terrible pain in the balls of my feet. I had to get up and put pressure on them. It had happened many times before and I would just get up and run around the room, then sit down and rub and massage them and maybe put some green liquid soap on the sore spots and massage until they relaxed and went back to normal. This time they both hurt—I needed to get up and tramp on the floor. In my hurry to get up my feet got tangled in the bed sheet and I went head first off the bed. My face crashed into my bed stand and my forearm and right knee hit the floor hard. I screamed in pain as I sat up on the floor and leaned on the side of the bed. My face hurt—I kept fishing, feeling for blood and there was none. I just knew there should be. The bed stand was tipped over—my clock and telephone were on the floor in the open closet. Kathy was calling "Mom, are you alright?" I managed to crawl to a chair and got up. My face hurt. I put a cold wet washcloth on it. It was 5:00 in the morning—too early to wake anyone else up. I quieted Kathy and we lay down and rested until 7:00. I knew my daughter in the big house would be up at seven as she had the grandchildren staying with them. Kathy and I live in the little house behind them which is a mother-in-law set up.

Sure enough the kids were up early. Deb came in to ask if we wanted doughnuts as she was going to make a run to the store. She was shocked when she looked at my face and immediately settled me in the big house on the couch with crushed ice on my sore spots and hot chocolate drink with peppermint and whipped cream, three great grandkids and a special cartoon to watch while she dashed out to get us doughnuts. Even though I didn't like what I saw in the mirror, and I knew I'd be black and blue and have to face the public, it was worth the pain and discomfort to get all the loving attention from my daughter and her family.

STORY THIRTY

Quaker Oats Man

When I was around seven or eight years old, I remember getting ready for school and hearing my older sister, Loretta, calling, "Oatmeal is ready on the breakfast table!" We were always hungry and listening for her call. Sometimes she'd say that Cream of Wheat was ready or cornmeal or mush or Wheatena or even fried cornmeal mush with maple syrup. We were always ready for something hot to eat on those cold winter mornings after we were dressed and ready for school.

I liked the oatmeal the best. I think the Quaker Oats Man has been around forever. My mom said that the oatmeal mush was the first solid food that I ate. It seemed to stick to my stomach and keep my whole body warm as I played along the snow banks on my way to school where the snow plow pushed the snow off the sidewalk. There seemed to be all kinds of oatmeal around when I was little. Some you had to cook and stir a long time. It was called steel-cut. Another was called rolled oats.

After I got married and moved out to California with my husband, Ken, and our three kids, Jim, Deby and Kathy, who showed up at our breakfast table? The Quaker Oats Man was here too! Not only would our kids enjoy the oatmeal for breakfast, but they were making oatmeal cookies every chance they got! They loved oatmeal! Then our grandchildren and our great-grandchildren ate with the Oat Man. In the winter, they ate hot oatmeal and in the summer, cold oat cereal. Our kids changed but the Oat Man never did!

My favorite way to have my morning oatmeal now is cooked thin with extra milk and brown sugar. I drink it on my way out the door in the morning in my favorite mug! I have loved my Quaker Oats Man for a very long time and so will my family for many years to come! You could say I've had a secret love affair with another man! I never confessed this one to my husband.

STORY THIRTY-ONE

The Chester Stewart Family

I, Carmel, was born on a farm in Onaway, Michigan, to Ethel and Chester Stewart on June 15, 1921. I was the youngest of five children. My dad's older brothers had all gone to the Gold Rush in Alaska. Dad decided to take his family out to Santa Rosa, California, because his cousins who lived there said that he could find work. Dad didn't like working on the farm so he finally sold it and drove west.

It was a long drive with the family. They would stop at different farms and buy chickens, milk, eggs, vegetables and fruit. Mom did the cooking over a fire or our camp stove. They would pitch our tent along the road or sometimes in the yard at a farmer's house. We finally settled in Hermosa Beach, California. We only stayed there for a short while then Dad decided to take his family back to Michigan. He hadn't found the work he had expected and didn't like the weather, and Mom missed her family.

Dad's sister, Ella, and her husband, Mac McTiver, lived in northern Michigan. Mac wrote to dad and told him that there was plenty of lumbering or logging going on in Newberry, Michigan. They lived on a big cattle farm. Uncle Mac worked in the woods at a lumber camp during the week and his brother Ray and Aunt Ella ran the farm. He told Dad to come help with the farm until he found a job with the lumber camps. This sounded good to Dad and Mom so they packed up the touring car and kids and went back to northern Michigan.

Going back was pretty rough—Mom and Dad and five kids in an older touring car. I was told that I sat on a little red chair between my mother's knees and the other kids sat in the back seat with all of our clothes and belongings. Our fenders and running boards carried our tent, blankets, food and camp stoves. We set up our tent in parks or campgrounds. We bathed in the lakes or rivers. Mom did all of the cooking—even fried doughnuts, pancakes, and fried cornmeal mush. I understand that something under the hood of the car caught fire while driving and Dad pulled the car over by the side of the road. He beat the fire out with an empty flour sack. Mom and my brother set up the tent back in the woods. Dad worked on the car. A campfire was built by my brother, Sterling, after we kids scrambled around and found dry branches. Then Mom had biscuits and milk gravy for dinner. We probably had flapjacks for breakfast. Dad fixed the car and we repacked it and then went on our way. We had the snap-on celluloid window curtain. We usually had them off for fresh air but if it rained we'd have to stop and each of the older kids would get out and start snapping the windows on to keep dry. I think the trip was hectic for our parents but we kids had a great time.

We stayed with Uncle Mac and Aunt Ella until Dad finally found work at a lumber camp near by our new home. Now the older kids could finally go to school. Loretta was thirteen, Ella was nine, Sterling was seven, and Viva was five. They could walk across the field to the little red schoolhouse. Mom could care for me, the baby, and helped Aunt Ella with the house. Soon Dad moved us into town quite close to the grammar school where it was easier for Mom to care for us. Dad could ride to the lumber camp on Monday morning on the caboose on the end of the train and ride back home Friday night and stay for the weekend. We missed him during the week but the weekends were the best! He would take us to the Two Heart River and teach us to fish and pick berries. We ate the fish and Mom canned the berries and made jams and jellies. Sometimes Dad would take us to the lumber camp and we would have dinner after the lumberjacks finished theirs. Of course the "Cook-ee" would let us ring the bell or hit a piece of iron from the railroad track with a hammer, or we could blow a long horn to call the men in to dinner. He took us camping on Perch Lake where we would swim and fish. When he came home on Fridays he always had something in his pockets for us, depending on the season. In the fall he'd have beechnuts from a squirrel's nest, or honey comb from a beehive. He always had wild meat like deer, rabbit, squirrel, partridge or fish.

Mom would get the older kids off to school and then she'd set up her pedal sewing machine and sew our clothes or sew for the public. She could make anything. She'd cut out her own patterns from newspaper. She made dresses, coats and even hats. She became the "Dressmaker or Tailor for the town." She could cook and bake too. She made the best biscuits and doughnuts.

She taught Loretta to cook and Ella helped her sew. Sterling kept the fires going and chopped and stacked the wood. Then he filled the wood box. Not only did he keep the fire going in the wood stove, but the pot-bellied stove that kept the rest of the house warm. We would dress behind the pot-bellied stove in the morning. We also played games behind the stove where it was warm as it was too cold to go outside. Sterling would get up early in the morning and light the fire to take the chill off the house before anyone else got up. If it rained or snowed and was too cold to go outside, Mom would get out the worn-out sheets and have us tear strips and roll them for bandages. We would also cut squares for patching and tore the rest into thin strips for crocheting rugs for the floor. We darned holes in stockings and made mittens out of Dad's worn-out wool socks. We rarely threw anything away. We passed dresses down to the next daughter when the oldest outgrew them. I was the youngest of four girls so a dress was pretty worn out by the time it got to me. It too went in the rag bag to be stripped for rug-making.

One of our cousins, Bernard McTiver, had to move his family to another small town so he let us move into his house which was in a better neighborhood and close to the elementary school. We were in the house for several years and then moved further up the hill by the high school. Dad's old farm in Onaway, Michigan, where I was born came back to him as the new owners hadn't paid the taxes. Dad paid the taxes, fixed it up again, and resold it for a good price. Dad was then able to buy a good lot and he and his son-in-law, Reinard Hemkis, built a beautiful home for Mom and Dad. We kids were all grown and off to college by then.

Ken Mullen, my husband, and I went back to Newberry to get married, and also visited several other times. We were traveling with the Ice Capades Ice Show when my Dad got sick with cancer. We flew home from London, England and were able to be with him for a few days before he died. Mom was in that house on McMillan Avenue until she too got sick with cancer and had to move closer to Ella and Vi, who both lived in Lower Michigan. She was 85 years old when she died. My brother died when he was in his sixties, and Loretta at 99. She would have been 100 soon. Ella was 96 and Vi was 93. She would have been 94 the following month and I just turned 91. I'm hoping to make 92 next June.

STORY THIRTY-TWO

Small Town Excitement

I remember one time when I was about ten years old and living in Newberry, Michigan when my father, Chester Stewart, called my mother, Ethel, and all five of us kids together—Loretta, Ella, Sterling, Viva, and me, Carmel—into our front room, sat us down and told us that there was something bad going on down town the next day. He did not want any of us going near the Workers Hall until he "okayed" it. He said some strange men had been out to his lumber camp in the woods and talked to his workers in the bunk house where they lived. Dad's men were very upset because the strangers wanted them to join the workers union. Dad told us that he made the strangers leave and stay off his camp's property until he checked in town to see what was going on. It seems that the non-union workers and industry owners were upset too as there were lots of logging and lumber mills and chemical plants in Newberry and their workers had been contacted by the strangers too. So the townspeople were getting together and were going to make them leave.

Early in the morning, I was told that a large group of loud, noisy, strange men came from all directions, gathering at the Workers Hall. Some men carried clubs and shovels and banged on the door of the Workers Hall and broke windows. The occupants scrambled to get out, yelling and screaming. They were very frightened! The townspeople arrived and they were ready too—with a bucket of tar and a bag of feathers. They chased the bad guys down the street and out of town. An older union man who seemed to be their leader was also chased and caught and they "tarred and feathered" him. We could only watch from our window as the others ran fast as they didn't like the looks of the tar and feathers. We were frightened too. We were also allowed to go out again. The riot hit the front page headlines of the Detroit newspaper and the Milwaukee Daily Journal. For a small town, we really had some excitement!

STORY THIRTY-THREE

Valentine's Day

Hurrah! Valentine's Day is here and I have my valentines all made. Our teacher had asked the class if anyone had a box at home that we could use for our valentine box. We could decorate it tomorrow and the other boys and girls could finish making their valentines and a few extra for decorating our school room. We will be having our Valentine's Day party on Friday. I was so excited—I raised my hand and told her I could bring a box. She said okay, she was depending on me to bring it all decorated. She also asked the class if they had any magazines, catalogs, or wallpaper scraps that they could bring so we could cut out flowers, birds, etc., to decorate our hand-made valentines. We could write little poems or sayings on our valentines if we wanted. They usually said the traditional "I love you" or the usual "you're nice" or the racy "hubba hubba". You needed to be selective in the messages of the valentines given to the boys in the class. No wrong signals should be given if you didn't like him or he thought you had a crush on him.

The only box I could find at home was our large Quaker Oats box which I didn't mind taking as I sort of had a crush on the Quaker Oats man's picture on the box anyway. I covered him and the rest of the box with white tissue paper and cut a long slot in the top. The teacher admired the box, even with its odd keg shape and gave it a special place on the corner of her desk. Every time someone put a valentine in I was filled with apprehension as I wondered if there would be one for me, as in those days the children didn't draw names or were not told to have valentines for everyone. What would happen if there wasn't even one?

The long awaited day arrived and I waited with breathless anticipation. The room was so beautifully decorated. Finally it was time to open the Valentines box. We had voted for two postmen to hand out the valentines. Everyone received at least two or three valentines. We had time to talk over our cards. The girls were giggling and the boys teasing. The teacher had made a Kool-Aid drink and lots of red valentine cookies. One boy, named Bill, said he like the card that I made for him and said "It was the best he got." I picked up the empty Quaker Oats Man box and hurried home, eager to read the rest of the messages. The first one I picked out was from Bill—and it was the best one I got.

STORY THIRTY-FOUR

My Life Experiences with Segregation

When I was little in the late 1920's, I grew up in a small town called Newberry, Michigan. It was a logging town in the Upper Peninsula. I didn't know the word "racism", but I sure sang like a racist. We would sing rhymes while jumping rope. In one of our songs we'd sing the "N" word. We also sang about others, like the Chinese person was called a "chink" and the Jewish people were called "kikes". We also had a Swede Town and a Finn Town. We didn't know the difference and worked and played together. After I graduated from high school in 1939, I got a job at a summer resort in a little town about 60 miles from home. It was an elegant resort with a nine-hole golf course, horseback riding along Lake Michigan, a swimming pool, and a lake for fishing or boating. They had two hotels with cabins and a huge dining room with a dance floor and band and bar. About a mile down the road was the crossroads for the main highway. Our resort had a hamburger restaurant on the corner.

If a Jewish family stopped in and asked about the resort and needed directions to see it, the manager would give them directions to get there, then he would immediately call the main office for reservations and warn them that a Jewish family was on their way. When they arrived they would tell them "Sorry, we're full." I was beginning to witness segregation and racism.

From there I moved to Detroit to live with my sister Ella and her husband George. Ella was a clothing or dress tailor and worked for the Singer Sewing Machine Company and they were making a new type of dress form that was shaped to your body. It was like a plaster of Paris covering cloth that was molded to your body, then dried and hardened and put on a stand so when you needed to fit a dress for yourself, you used your dress form for a good fit. My summer job was to assist Ella, however needed. I would travel by bus and go shop to shop all over Detroit and I had to sit in the front of the bus while the black people sat in the back. Black people could not eat in a white restaurant or drink from the same water fountain or even use the public restrooms.

Ella and George had a wonderful cleaning lady called LuLu. She cleaned, cooked meals, and took care of the kids, but because she was black she never sat at the dinner table. She always had her meals later in the kitchen by herself. She worked for them for many years, even after retirement. She was loved by the whole family.

I went to Grand Rapids to college for awhile and then World War II broke out so I was chosen to skate in the Ice Capades Ice Show. This is where I met and married Ken Mullen. I remember when we were skating in Pittsburgh, Pennsylvania, 1947, and were invited to a publicity party after opening night's show where we would meet the media, different celebrities, movie stars and professional athletes. I got to meet the famous legend Jackie Robinson, who was one of the pioneers to receive equal rights as an athlete. He was the first black player to be on a team and was still having a hard time being accepted by all the public. Ken and I were given tickets to a game so we were very fortunate to see him play. What an amazing athlete!

We finally left the Ice Capades to settle down in Fresno, California to raise our family. We had Jim, then five years later we had Deby, and another five and in 1960 we had Kathy, who has Down syndrome. In the early years we had it rough with Kathy being different. Then in 1969 our son Jim was severely beaten in a race riot in Roeding Park. These life experiences made our family stronger and opened our eyes to reach out to others. Everyone has the same prayer for their children to be accepted by the world and to have the opportunities to develop the gifts that God has given them with love and acceptance. Doors will open towards wonderful relationships and we should work towards integration, instead of segregation.

STORY THIRTY-FIVE

War Time

In 1941 I found myself living in Grand Rapids, Michigan with my sister Vi and her husband, Dick Matheson. World War II had broken out and women started working in factories as the men were being drafted to fight in the war. Most of the automobiles were manufactured at General Motors out of Detroit, Michigan, and many of their parts were manufactured in smaller cities around Detroit. These were now changed over to manufacture guns, bullets, etc. for the war. My brother-in-law hadn't been drafted yet as they had two small children in their family. He decided to sign up to work in the Saginaw Steering Gear Factory which was quite close to his home in Grand Rapids, Michigan. The factory was now making guns, ammunition, etc.

I had left college in Grand Rapids and gone home for awhile as I was asked to put on an ice show for the annual Newberry Winter Carnival. It was lots of fun and they paid me $700.00 which was a lot of money in those days.

I had heard that a traveling ice show, called the Ice Capades, was going to have auditions for their show in Chicago, Illinois, the following weekend. I mentioned it to my folks and they said if you want to audition, we will drive you there. I was so excited to try out.

My audition went quite well. I had to skate the figure eights first and lucky me, I had taken lessons in Sault Ste. Marie or Soo, Michigan, and learned most of them. You skate on a figure eight using your left foot and right foot. You have two edges on your blades—one inside edge and one outside edge—which enables you to turn right or left, forward or backward, twist or turn and spin and jump. You also learn to turn your head, arms, shoulders and body so everything works together for good form and good control. Then I had to do a short routine on the ice. I started out posing for the introduction of my music which was the "Waltz of the Flowers". After the introduction, I immediately whipped into a short two foot spin, skated forward with long strides, preparing for my three waltz jumps, which means jumping forward on the left foot and turning backward in the air, landing on the right edge, riding it out with turning your shoulders and head and repeating two more times. I continued with waltz edges and spirals across and around the ice. My stag jump was great and I ended with a camel spin, dropping into a fast sit spin. I wrapped my free foot around my spinning foot and as I did so, suddenly I lost my edge and fell on my butt, still spinning, but ended with the music, sprawled on the ice in my best pose in that position.

I felt real good about my short routine even though I fell. I filled out lots of papers and turned them in.

The man said they would let me know if they could use me by letter. I waited a few weeks and hadn't heard from them so I decided to go back to Grand Rapids as Dick had written that a lot of women were now working in the factories and I could stay with he and Vi and get a job there too. I took his advice and went back to Grand Rapids and got a job. I was working on the assembly line, putting thirty caliber bullets into the clips for thirty caliber rifles. The factory was called the Saginaw Steering Gear and they had been working on a system of mass-producing machine guns. Until them all machine guns were individually hand-made or crafted. Experts were skeptical and did not believe that machine guns could be assembled on an assembly line. Through innovation, stamina and skill, they proved it could be done. Saginaw Steering Gear Factory was able to test and deliver a completed machine gun more than seven months ahead of schedule. Several other factories were working on machine gun manufacturing, but our plant received the first order and was considered a pioneer in the field as of March 25, 1941. The Saginaw people were proud of their accomplishment in their plant.

I really enjoyed the time I spent in the factory. I liked the assembly work and met a lot of women who had never worked before. We carried our lunches every day and lived by the bells and clocks and learned to check in and out. I finally got a letter from the Ice Capades with a ticket to Hollywood, California. I had to get permissions to leave the factory as it was war time and everyone needed to help the cause. The ladies and I were very proud of the work we did there and that we could serve our country during the war and I thought of the service men and women as I rode the train to Hollywood to start my new adventure with the Ice Capades.

STORY THIRTY-SIX

Straits of Mackinac

My family lived in the Upper Peninsula of the state of Michigan. My grandparents and their families lived in the Lower Peninsula, which was divided by the Straits of Mackinac where Lake Michigan and Lake Huron flowed together. It was a five mile stretch of water and ice and a forty minute ride by ferry boat which carried our car and family across. We kids loved the trip to Grandma's. My mom got out the leftover roast beef from Sunday's dinner, got out the meat grinder, hooked it on the edge of the table, put chunks of meat in and turned the crank. The meat came out into a bowl and we added mustard and chopped pickles. She made lots of our favorite sandwiches and then boiled enough hard-boiled eggs for each of us and packed the salt and pepper. Sometimes she'd make a jar of lemonade to wash it down in our folding tin cups. Dad would get us up early in the morning for an early start as it was a long trip to St. Ignace where we would wait in line to drive on the ferry boat. Sometimes we would have to wait until late at night just to get on a ferry boat.

While waiting in a slow line of moving cars, we kids could get out and play with the other kids and run along with the cars. It was a ¼ mile walk to the closest comfort station by the dock entrance near the highway in Mackinaw City. There would be vendors trying to sell us dry smoked fish or pasties—folded crusts that contained ground beef, chopped potatoes, onions, rutabagas, carrots, pepper and gravy inside. They were delicious but we couldn't afford them often. We would save our picnic lunch until we got on the ferry and would take it to the waiting room upstairs after parking our car in the lower level. We always used salt on our boiled eggs as the Great Lakes were all fresh water and there was very little salt in the water or ground. We were always told to eat lots of salt or we would get a goiter on our neck.

On nice days we could walk all over the ferry and look out at all the little islands, especially Mackinaw Island, with the huge, elegant hotel. It is also known for not having any automobiles on the island. The only means of travel on the island are horse and buggy or bicycles. If the weather was bad in the winter time it was a little scarier. The ferry had to keep going, breaking through the ice. There were stories of ferries being frozen solid in the ice where the people had to get off with whatever they could carry and walk the rest of the way across, leaving their car on the frozen ferry.

One night the wind was blowing hard and the sleet (icy, cold rain) was coming down hard and would freeze as soon as it hit the deck. The icy floor was so slippery you could hardly stand up.

They tied a rope from the stairway to the waiting room so people could hang on to something to cross from one to the other.My brother Sterling, sister Viva and I made a human chain with our bodies for people to hang on to as well as the rope. We were cold and drenched but we didn't care, we were kids.

In November, 1957, the car ferry service between Mackinaw City and St. Ignace ended as they finally finished the five mile bridge over the straits. Driving over the new bridge is a blessing and a necessity as it was boosting the tourist travel and was more convenient for everyone, but the five mile ferry trip was a thrill of its own. I loved it!

STORY THIRTY-SEVEN

Traveling by Train

Trains were quite a big part of my life. As a little girl we lived near the railroad tracks. I used to play on the tracks with my sister Viva and brother Sterling almost every day. The trains seemed to run on the tracks early in the morning and again in the evening so we didn't have to worry about getting hurt or being hit by a train during the day. We played games like who could walk on one track the longest without falling off or who could jump straight up and land back on the track. We were using it as our balance beam.

The springtime was when the wild strawberries would ripen along the railroad on a mound of dirt along the railroad track. The wild strawberries grew on the sunny side of the mound or hill. We would fill our little containers with berries and then sit on the track to devour them. When we finished we would continue playing by hopping on the logs or ties down the middle of the track.

When we were in the house we knew what time the train would go by and we would run out to the front yard to wave to the engineer in the front car and then wait to wave to the man in the caboose. My dad was a lumberjack and in charge of several lumber camps. Sometimes he would take us out to visit the camp and have dinner there. He would make arrangements for us to ride in the caboose where we could sit with the man in charge of switching the tracks when the train had to branch off in a different direction. We sat way up high on benches in a tiny room where we could look out a tiny window. We might see a deer with her fawn or a black bear moseying along the tracks. Another time dad took my sister Vi and I with him on the "speeder" to pick up my brother Sterling and his friend who had been camping on the river near the lumber camp. They had fished for rainbow trout and set traps for wild game like rabbits, foxes and flying squirrels. The speeder was like a golf cart and was pumped by two bars across from each other by two men. They would push and pull the bars back and forth to make it go down the railroad tracks. We went in the evening after the regular train had cleared the tracks to enjoy the quiet early evening when the birds and animals would be settled down. The stars and moon came out to light our way. We would sleep on blankets in the office at the camp, eat a quick breakfast in the morning, gather the boys and head for home. We really had to watch for deer that might be crossing the track.

When I was going to high school I was really interested in figure skating at our ice rink. I could take the train to my cousin's house in Sault Ste. Marie (better known as Soo, Michigan), which was only 60 or 70 miles from my home.

I would stay at my cousin's house where I could take figure skating lessons. The first time I went, I seemed to catch on and loved it, so every time I had any days away from school, I would head for the train and Soo, Michigan, for my lessons. The train was there when I was a child and it carried me into my future of an ice skating profession and meeting my husband.

STORY THIRTY-EIGHT

Train Travel

My sister Ella had left home and she had gone to Detroit, Michigan, to a beauty school where she met and married George Hafferkamp. I now had another place to go and continue my ice skating instructions. I had been invited to other little towns close to home like Munising, Manistique, and the Soo, Michigan, to skate exhibitions between periods at the hockey games. I liked it and wanted to learn more so I went to Detroit where I learned more dancing, jumps and spins that they used in figure skating on ice. I had already learned most of the figure eights and basics that I needed. To get there I would have to ride the train all the way to Detroit by myself. I had ridden by car many times to the Lower Peninsula to visit my grandmother, aunts, uncles and cousins, but never went as far south as Detroit.

I really enjoyed the train ride. I could watch out the window and see wild deer, beautiful pine trees and swamp land with lots of wild blue flags or iris flowers.

We followed the rivers that flowed and were a rusty red color from all of the copper and iron in the ground. Then we arrived at the Straits of Mackinaw. It was late fall and I had never crossed the straits on a train before. I had heard of the train ferry boats and how they would plow their way through the ice and sometimes become frozen where they could not go on and passengers could either get off the train ferry and walk over the frozen water to Mackinaw City or wait for the other ferry boat to come and break them loose. We didn't have any trouble at all. The train tracks went out on the dock and switched on to the tracks on the ferry. We could stay with the train or go upstairs to the upper deck or waiting room. It took us 40 minutes to get to the other side. When the train got off the ferry and started to go through Mackinaw City, everything seemed to change. I saw lots of farm land with apple, peach and cherry orchards, and lots of vegetable gardens and cattle farms. Now the cities were bigger and had more stores for shopping. I was fascinated with it all. My sister met me at the train station and we took a bus to her home in the city. I traveled those tracks quite often during my high school days and also after I graduated and then went to college in Grand Rapids.

After joining Ice Capades, I traveled across the country from Grand Rapids to California. It was such fun to see the changes in the different states and the beautiful flowers, mountains, valleys and the children waving to us on the train just as I had done back in Newberry. When we arrived in Los Angeles and I opened the curtains on the train, I'll never forget the beauty of the bright sunshine on the flowers and palm trees and homes like I had never seen before. How flat and rambling the houses were!

I stayed in a boarding house with lots of rooms and we all ate our meals together in a dining room. We had the new show rehearsals every day. Picture calls and costumes to try on. Then we rode on the train to our home for vacation, then on to Atlantic City for more new show rehearsals. We took a train from city to city, some in a passenger train with sleepers or compartment trains. I loved it all. I was single while traveling for four years.

We were riding on a sleeper train with bunk beds and four of the girls were going to teach me to smoke cigarettes as most of them did already. So the four of us crawled into a lower bunk and snapped the curtains shut. We had about two feet of space over our heads, which almost touched the ceiling as the upper bunk was directly above. One of the girls lit up her cigarette, then another and another, and then it was my turn. The little room was full of smoke. They told me how to take a little puff, and then blow it out my nose. I swallowed that puff and I choked and coughed and thought I was going to die. I fought to find the snapped curtains—I wanted out of there! Our little closed bunk was blue with smoke and I couldn't find the opening. I finally opened it and stumbled out just gasping for air. I coughed some more and finally calmed down. To this day, I've never smoked again. From then on I always requested a top bunk where the curtains never reached the ceiling. I've always loved traveling by train. After Ken and I got married we usually had compartments which were more private and had our own sink and toilet. When our son Jim was born they warmed his bottle in the dining car and when he was a toddler we put a small carton of milk inside the water coolers at the end of our coach. We carried small individual boxes of dry cereal so we could feed him something before the dining car opened.

I learned so much traveling by train. We always had four or five railroad cars just for our staff, with boys in one and girls in another. Of course we moved back and forth to play games or cards and visited. I learned to play poker and other card games. I also learned to knit baby clothes, scarves and sweaters. I crocheted purses and a bed spread. We learned how to act like ladies and gentlemen. In those days we couldn't wear pants or slacks in public. We would wear our slacks on the train in our cars but when we arrived at our destination, we would roll our pant legs up, put on our high heels, and then wear a long coat so it would look like we were wearing dresses and heels as we got off the train. The media was usually waiting for us with their cameras and publicity interviews.

I can still hear the sound of the iron wheels going round and round on the iron railroad tracks. I loved that sound. I want to do it again.

STORY THIRTY-NINE

A Day at the Ice Rink

I was teaching a Special Olympics Ice Skating group at the ice rink here in Fresno. The ice rink donated the ice a couple of hours once a week so the special education students and their teachers from several schools showed up for skating lessons. After putting on their skates we taught the students to walk on the floor, and then do some exercising on the floor to warm up their muscles. We'd also have them sit on the floor and show them how to roll over on their hands and knees and then stand straight up so that if they fell on the ice they would know how to get back up. I too had my skates on but my blades have covers on them called skate guards. They are to keep my blade edges sharp. You have two edges on your blade called inside and outside edges. The edges have to be razor sharp so they can cut into the ice and keep your blades from sliding our from under you.

Once the students stand on the ice they want to hold on the wall and just walk or side step.

That's where they really get the feel of the ice and find their balance. We have them march in place, shifting their weight from one foot to the other. Then you take one hand while holding them under their shoulder. You march them out onto the ice with their toes turned out. A little glide makes the momentum carry them forward so they are using their inside edges to push off into a stroke. They find they are skating forward and then you gradually let go of their hand and they are skating.

One day after I had finished working with them on the hard rubber floor, we all headed for the ice. I was talking to one of the students and as we were about to step onto the ice when some of the students who already knew how to skate stepped out onto the ice and started to skate around and around the arena. I needed to get with them right away so I quickly stepped into the flow of traffic on the ice. Also it was another time for me to show off my skills. When I stepped forward to join them, I was stopped dead in my tracks! I still had my guards on my blades, and my skate slipped sideways! I smacked hard on the ice, hitting my face and oh, how it hurt! I felt like lying down and putting my face on that cold ice to help it feel better. How embarrassing! I had to sit there and take off both guards before I could get up. Luckily one of the teachers had gone for an ice bag. I had just had cataract surgery a couple of days earlier so after I got off the ice I went to my doctor to check my eye! My eye was okay but it didn't take long before I looked like a boxer who'd just taken a beating! I had bruises on my cheek and the blackest black eye for a couple of weeks!

Here is a note of advice: Remember that verse in the Bible—
"Pride goes before a fall?" Well, I was prideful and I did fall! And
here is a second note of advice: "Don't forget to take your skate
guards off!"

STORY FORTY

An Exciting Day

We were having a nice quiet Saturday afternoon in June, 1980. The chores had already been finished and everyone was enjoying free time. Steve had gone fishing with his dad. Deby and her friend Linda had planned on an early movie. Deby was getting ready in her room when she noticed a canker sore on her lip. She called to me and asked: "What can I put on a sore on my lip?" I told her there was a tube of salve in the junk drawer in the kitchen just for canker sores if she thought that was her problem. "Put a little on your finger and wipe it across your lips."

She said she found it so I didn't pay much attention to her. She had called Linda and Linda told her to put on some baking soda. Then I heard her shout again. This time she sounded like she was frightened. "Mom, my lips are burning!"

I ran to the kitchen asking—"what did you use?" She showed me the tube. It wasn't the lip salve. It was a tube from the veterinarian and it had a crazy name that I didn't recognize. "Deby, your lips are white and they're swelling.

Where is the telephone book?"

Linda had arrived so I asked her to call the veterinary center. Deby had already jumped up on the side of the sink, hanging her head and mouth over the water spigot so the water could wash over her lips. Linda finally got the vet center. She spelled out the name on the tube and told them Deby had put it on her lips. They said to call the Poison Control Center as they only took care of dogs.

It took forever to get through to the Poison Control Center. We were so frightened as Deby looked horrible. She looked like she had been hit in the mouth with a wild pitch. Her lips were huge and white from the baking soda. I took the phone and I finally was able to tell them our problem. They said to relax and they would look it up in their records. He was laughing as the medicine turned out to be salve for our dog, Duke, and was supposed to be put on his testicles for a bad itch. Deby's directions were to keep rinsing her lips with water every fifteen minutes until the itch went away and to make Linda promise to never, ever tell this story to their friends.

STORY FORTY-ONE

Atlantic and Pacific Oceans

I've really enjoyed the oceans ever since I joined the Ice Capades Ice Show in Los Angeles in 1941. We skated at the Pan Pacific Auditorium, skating the 1941 ice show in the evenings and also rehearsing the new 1942 show in the mornings. With free time we could go to the beach or drive up and down the coast, visiting different spots along the way. We saw the Hearst Castle when you could walk through the whole castle in one visit and also see the wild animals that were fenced off surrounding the property. We went to the Santa Monica "Muscle Beach" where all of the weightlifters worked out and all of the rides were out on the pier. At the end of our stay in Los Angeles we had two weeks of vacation and then went on to Atlantic City to rehearse more at the Convention Hall on the boardwalk along the beach on the Atlantic Ocean.

I love the oceans. We sun-bathed, dove through the waves and rode the waves to the shore. In the early years we could watch great entertainment on the end of the pier.

There were lots of vaudeville acts and even a horse that dove, or jumped, off the diving platform into the ocean. One time one of our skaters, Harry Hasley, had the job of watching a huge balloon that was tied to the boardwalk with a rope cable that advertised our Ice Capades show and the dates that we'd be there. He tied it up every morning and took it down in the evening. One day the wind was so strong that the boss said he better take it down early. Harry was trying to untie it from the boardwalk. All of a sudden it broke loose. Harry hung on to his cable with all his strength as he didn't want to lose the balloon that he was responsible for. The wind was so strong, carrying Harry half-running and dangling off the boardwalk, through the people sunning on the beach, and out over the ocean. When he passed the end of the pier he finally let go, dropping off and falling into the ocean. A lifeguard from the pier dove in and picked him up. We all laughed when we saw that Harry was okay and so did the boss. I guess we lost the balloon as we never saw it again.

After Ken and I were married we skated five more years and then we started raising a family. We already had Jim with us and Jim needed to be in school. We settled in Fresno, California, which isn't too far from the west coast near the Pacific Ocean. We drove there often. We loved Muscle Beach, the boardwalk, and the parks with lots of swings and rides. Roller skating and bike parks—we used them all.

At one time Ken was offered a job at a hotel in Westchester, California, close to the ocean. We decided to rent our house in Fresno and move to the coast. We stayed for a year and a half. Our biggest worry was—which beach should we go to today?

Our neighbors, Pat and Al Shell and their kids, were great. They loved the ocean too. Ken and Al would go to their work every day and join us in the evening. Pat and I and the kids would head for one of the beaches. We ate lots of hot dogs, cookies and usually had two thermos jugs full of hot soup. Ken worked long hours and missed his family so we moved back to Fresno. Again Ken was working for the Tropicana or Hacienda Hotel. Our family had grown with Jim, Deby and Kathy, so we again went to the ocean often. People would lend us their motor home or beach house. One time Ken only had time off to go for a weekend. Some of the kids on the beach had a large wooden saucer that they'd run and hop on and slide in the water. Ken was going to show us how to ride it. He threw it out, ran a few steps, and jumped on—the board slipped out and threw Ken up in the air, landing him on his shoulder. We had it checked and found it was broken. We thought we'd have to go home but then Ken called his boss and he told Ken to take two weeks off as he wouldn't be able to work anyway. Lucky us, Ken was slowed down with his arm in a sling but he still enjoyed walking on the beach and fishing from the pier.

Later we started renting the Dahl's house. They were friends who had a beach house to rent. We automatically reserved it for the first week in August every year. It was near Cayucos in Morro Bay. We usually had our Thanksgiving there. I just heard that the kids, grandkids, and great grandkids are all planning on having Thanksgiving at the Dahl's house at the beach this year, 2013.

STORY FORTY-TWO

Few Days in the Mountains

I wondered if I would enjoy a four day trip to the mountains at Bass Lake at this time in my life. This is September 15, 2013. I am 92 years old and have just lost my 52 year-old daughter, Kathy, who had Down syndrome. Will I just be lonely? Will I be able to remember to take my medication? How far is the bathroom from my bed? What if I have an accident? Will I be too slow to keep up with the others? Can I say "no" again? I have no more excuses. I'll go. Liz will pick me up on Monday. I've known Liz for a long time. I've been to her cabin at Bass Lake with my family many times but I was younger then—and it will just be Liz and me this time. Oh well, I've committed.

Liz picked me up bright and early Monday morning. We had a nice chatty visit on the way. As we drove up Highway 41 through the foothills, I started to reminisce to Liz when we passed the water springs on the way to the little settlement of O'Neals, California. Jim was a baby—he's now 62. My husband, Ken, Jim and I had friends—the Vanderburgs—who ran the store at O'Neals crossing.

We'd go there to visit for the weekend and enjoy square danc-ing, fishing in the lake nearby, and riding around looking at old mines. Ken would go hunting with Harry and I'd mind the store with Florence, her daughter and Jim. Liz listened as I chatted on about camping with my family under the stars at Bass Lake—no tent, just the blanket we slept on, a fry pan and pot to cook in and our bathing suits. I was enjoying myself already and Liz seemed to enjoy herself too.

We arrived at Liz's house which was in a little retirement village in a small valley with houses surrounded with flowers, shrubs, and pine trees. The air was so fresh, cool, and smelled of pine needles. I felt at home already. In back of Liz's house she had a huge back yard with a patio filled with picnic tables, a golf cart and a trailer for her motor boat. It was getting close to dinner time so Liz led me to a beautiful bedroom with a bathroom next door and told me to settle in and then meet her on the front porch where she was greeting neighbors as they walked by. They were all so friendly as they visited and contin-ued their evening walk around the village. As we were visiting on the porch a beautiful young deer—a doe—came out of the woods and nibbled on Liz's flowers just a few feet below the porch where we were sitting. Liz went back to the kitchen and came back with hotdogs and the trimmings, plus fruit and hash browns and ice tea for us to enjoy as we left Fresno's heat behind us. We watched the dancers on television that night.

The next morning we shopped for a few groceries and then went down to the dock where her boat was tied. We had a lus-cious salad for lunch, rode around the shore of the lake in the golf cart, and then drove to a place where Liz wanted to put her ashes when she passed away in the future. I was surprised to visit such a special place where they left gold plates glued on the rocks with names and dates. There was also a path up the mountain, through the pine trees with ten steps to the cross, with Bible verses on each step. We went to the famous Elderberry House for dinner which I really enjoyed with spinach soup, bass with all the trimmings and dessert served in the garden. The last day was spent on the lake in Liz's motorboat where we saw two eagles sitting in their nest on the top of a tree along the shore. We finished the day off with ice cream cones at Miller's store by Ducey's Lodge.

Liz was a great host and a very dear friend. I had such a great time and am looking forward to more trips to Bass Lake.

STORY FORTY-THREE

The 117th Rose Parade

A few years ago our daughter Kathy was nominated and chosen to ride on a float in the Rose Parade in Pasadena, California on January 2, 2006. She was chosen to ride on the float of the Kiwanis Club from Fresno, California. The theme of the float was "storybook characters". We decided to dress Kathy as a princess wearing a beautiful gold jacket, black velvet pants and an elegant gold crown on her head. Her sister Deby decided to drive Kathy and me to Pasadena for the weekend. The weather was reported to be cold with heavy rainstorms so we took our heavy plastic raincoats, snow pants and rain boots. We also took a plastic jacket and pants for Kathy that we ended up putting on under her gold jacket and fancy pants.

We arrived on Friday night and checked in at our hotel and had dinner at Mimi's Restaurant. We went to bed early so we knew we had a busy two days ahead of us. We got up early and grabbed our umbrellas as it was raining lightly. We had to check in at a church and get our instructions.

We met the people in charge who told us where Kathy would be sitting on the float. We had a short meeting and then all float riders were taken to lunch. Deby and I and other parents went to the same restaurant but were sitting at a different table. Kathy was a little nervous at their table and Deby was invited to sit with her and she settled down. After lunch we were all taken in the rain to some huge open air warehouses where the floats were parked getting some last minute roses added for the beautiful parade on Sunday. We found our Kiwanis float. It was beautiful. Kathy was shown where she would be sitting among the roses and then we were free to wander through all the warehouses and watch the owners give their floats last minute changes. Even though it was raining, the smell of the roses and the beauty and hard work of getting ready for the pageant was overwhelming. We had dinner and went to bed early as Kathy had to be dressed and at the church at 6:00 in the morning.

We had a nice breakfast close to the church. It was raining so we opened our umbrellas and ran to the church. We had another quick meeting. We were told that they would be responsible for our kids from then on and we could pick them up at the church after the parade finished. It was raining harder so we put Kathy's rain pants on under her black dress pants and plastic jacket under her gold jacket. They said they possibly would wear plastic raincoats if the parade people approved. They had already ordered them. We left Kathy with her group and went to our car. The streets were so roped off for the parade the traffic was terrible. Deby parked the car in a garage parking lot. We had to walk about 15 blocks to our seats in the bleachers.

Deby parked the car in a garage parking lot. We had to walk about 15 blocks to our seats in the bleachers. It was raining harder and we already were wearing our snow pants, heavy jackets with hoods and waterproof heavy tennis shoes. Deby also carried a blanket to sit on as we had tickets to sit in the bleachers on the corner where all floats stopped or paused for the media. We found our seats and were told not to lose our tickets as if we left our seats and wanted to go back we'd have to show the tickets each time. Volunteers were wiping rain off the benches at first but then the rain came down harder and it was useless. By that time the crowds were more congested and the cold wind was blowing harder. The chairs were lined up both sides of the street. There were so many people walking in both directions that you couldn't use umbrellas. They'd bump each other or the wind would blow them inside out. The rain came down so heavy we put our raincoats on and snapped our hoods around our face and neck. We were sitting in water. Our blanket was saturated. Deby tried to fold it up and in doing so she dropped her seat ticket under the bleachers. She could see it on the ground. We were sitting almost to the top of the bleachers. She took off to get the ticket. They had a hot chocolate stand close to the bleachers. Luckily Deby is a gymnast as there was a fence surrounding the bleachers. Deby climbed over and retrieved her ticket. She brought us some hot chocolate—it was cold and the box was wet and flimsy and useless, but we drank it anyway.

The parade had started. I guess it was wonderful. Everyone sitting had their umbrellas open and it was hard to see. The downpour kept coming.

The marchers were wearing raincoats. I worried about Kathy—was she miserable? Was she soaking wet and as cold as we were? Her float arrived and it was beautiful. She was beautiful. She didn't mind the rain. She was smiling at the crowd, waving her special wave, then waving her "I Love You" sign, enjoying every minute, rain or shine. We watched and the parade went on. When it was almost over we fought the crowd getting down from the bleachers.

We finally headed for our car in the garage. People were everywhere slopping through the water. It was over your shoe tops as you tried to cross a street. You had to walk through it—slop, slop. We finally got to the garage. We stripped off our wet plastic clothes, then the rest of our clothes—even our snow pants as we were soaked to the skin. We pulled on some dry pants (no dry underwear), and we were so very cold. We were finally out of the garage and going. It felt so good. The roads were roped off and we had to find our way around them. We finally got to the church but it was locked. We had to wait in our car in pouring rain until someone came over and unlocked the door. The church was so cozy and warm when we finally got in. Kathy's group finally arrived. They were all drenched but happy. They were all looking for the bathroom and wanted to get their wet clothes off. They were soaked to the skin, icy cold, but happy as larks. I guess they had a wonderful time together on the float during the parade. All good things do have to end. Kathy put her dry clothes on and her warm dry jacket and joined her new friends to discuss all the happy times, even though they were sitting in wet, wilted, beautiful roses, waving to family and friends in Pasadena and all over the world. We took more pictures, said thank you and headed for home.

We heard that a snowstorm was heading to the Grapevine over the mountain so we took off for home. We beat the storm and stopped in Bakersfield for a hot meal. We got home and found they too had had a heavy rainstorm that flooded one bedroom! The Rose Parade was one great memory of fun and adventure that will be cherished forever.

STORY FORTY-FOUR

A Day to Myself

The day started out beautifully. The sun was shining, not much wind blowing, and the pool at Break the Barriers was nice and warm. Usually I dreaded taking off my robe as the cold fall wind would blow on me as I walked down the long ramp to enter the warm water in the pool. Today was wonderful. The aqua aerobics program was refreshing and the workout great. The women involved were cheerful and ready. When we finished, I hurriedly ran up the ramp, dried my body, tied my towel around my waist, put my robe on over the towel, and rushed out to my warm car which was parked in the sunshine. I decided to treat myself to breakfast at McDonald's which included a sausage burrito and a senior cup of hot McDonald's coffee—all for $1.72. I consumed it on the way home and then ran into my house for a quick shower. The girls at the pool had been talking about Charming Charlie's jewelry store in Fashion Fair mall. My time was my own—no responsibilities today—so I decided to check it out.

The store was fascinating. There were lots of things in every corner—earrings, necklaces, scarves, belts and shoes. I found what I needed and as I was going to my car I noticed Penney's around the corner. I decided to go over and look for a long-sleeved blouse or sweater. It would only take a short time. I found a parking place close to the side entrance to Penney's right near where the petite sizes were and found a long-sleeved pink sweater immediately. It was marked down from $24.00 to $12.00 as they were having a big sale. I was curious to see what else they had on sale. I moseyed around, carrying the pink sweater. I then found myself in the junior department. I ran into a friend of my daughter Kathy's and talked to her for a long time. I noticed she was carrying a bag from Macy's and then I saw a Macy's sign where the mall walkway crossed the Penney's store. My friend left and I walked on down the mall to the shoe department, stopping off to look in the sportswear department, then on to the shoes. I tried on several pairs. I still had the pink sweater on a hanger and it kept falling off the boxes where I stacked it while trying on the shoes. I couldn't find a clerk so I left the shoes. I saw some fancy scarves so I went over there and walked around, looking for different ways to tie the scarves over a dress or sweater. A large group of young men were doing something down the mall that caused them to shout or chant loudly every once in a while. I was getting tired and wasn't quite sure of where I was on the mall. I decided to go to a cashier, pay for my sweater, and head back down the mall to my car. I looked around—I couldn't remember where Shaw Avenue was. I found a cashier, got in line and looked at my phone to check the time. It said 6:00. I couldn't believe it. I thought it was about 2:00 or 3:00 at the most.

STORY FORTY-FIVE

Fun on the Farm

I don't remember too much of the first few years of my life. I do remember stories from my siblings and pictures of all of us over those years. I do remember climbing on our bunk beds with my siblings in our little house. We lived by the bridge of the Tahquamenon River in northern Michigan in the early 1920's. I also remember when we lived with and played in the parlor of Aunt Ella's and Uncle Mack's house. They had a huge bear fur rug on the floor with head attached. We would listen and dance to the wind-up big horn Victrola. They also had a big porch that almost surrounded their house with a huge porch swing. This is where we played when it rained. They had an indoor water pump in the kitchen and wood burning stove with a big boiler or tub that was full of hot water for cooking, washing dishes, or washing clothes. It also heated the kitchen and dining room. I also remember Aunt Ella's creamed peas and little fresh potatoes. She grew her own garden and when the potatoes were young and tender she would dig some up and put them in a pail of water. The children's job was to stir them with a stick which took the tender skins off so she didn't have to peel the potatoes before cooking. She would also have us shuck the peas out of their pods. To keep us busy and out of her way when she was tending her garden, Aunt Ella would have us pick the potato bugs off the leaves of the potato plants. Then we would make cookies and use the bugs for raisins. We did a lot of pretending and make-believing when we played at her house. There was a garden, chickens and turkeys in the back of the house. The cow barn was across the road where they fed and milked the cows and stored the hay. The pig pen was outside the barn. My brother's job was to slop the pigs or feed them the slop or left-overs of garbage. They seemed to eat everything or anything you gave them— even if it was in the mud. The McTivers not only provided the town with milk, cream and eggs, but their son, Mike, also cut ice from a pond or lake near their property. He stored it in their icehouse with layers of sawdust from Uncle Mack's sawmill to keep it frozen. He delivered the ice to families for their iceboxes which were the refrigerators in those days. They also had a horse barn for the work houses that would pull their ice wagon. Later when we moved in to town to go to school, we kids just loved to visit the farm. We could play in the hay barn—swing from a rope in the rafters and land in the hay. We could carry our quilts or blankets to the barn and sleep out in the sweet-smelling hay. We would tell ghost stories until it got dark and play till we got tired and finally went to sleep. We loved it. We had great times without store-bought toys, game boys or video games. We really knew how to play!

STORY FORTY-SIX

Sensuous Seniors 1990

What a great year 1989 was for me and eleven other chosen women. I was dancing at a Special Olympics dance, celebrating one of the sports events, when I was approached by a lady involved in a beauty school here in Fresno. She wondered if I would be interested in joining a group of women whose pictures would be in a "Sensuous Seniors 1990 Calendar"-a calendar of 12 glamorous women between the ages of 50 and 73, still working, healthy, with positive attitudes and enjoying life after 50. Of course I was flattered and decided to give it a try.

The year began. We had our pictures taken by a special professional photographer who made us look so glamorous, sensuous, and pretty. We also were interviewed for a brief biography of our lives. The calendar was put together. I turned out to be Miss February with a picture of me with my ice skates draped over my shoulder. We appeared at Gottschalk's for modeling their clothing and autographing our calendars. We also modeled clothes at J C Penney Department Store.

We traveled to Los Angeles to be interviewed by the media there. Naomi Gibbs, Miss September, and I were invited to join the Phil Donahue Show on Monday, November 27, 1989. Naomi decided to go early with her daughter, so I ended up going by myself. My daughter and some of our family relations and friends made the beginning of my trip very interesting and fun. The airport was very busy. I was checking in my bags. Deby talked to the clerk and he handed her the microphone, saying "This young lady has an announcement to make." Deby said: "This lady, my mother, is going to be on the Phil Donahue Show on November 2ih as she is Miss February in a sexy granny calendar. Be sure to watch!" My face was so red. Deby had given me her purse to hold and in my embarrassment I carried it with me on the plane. She realized where it was just as the plane was ready to take off and got permission to run out and get on the plane just in time to grab it and go.

The plane trip was great, everyone was curious, and I had plenty of calendars to hand out. We got to New York and I had been instructed to go to the baggage department where I would meet a man from the Donahue Show to take me to the Drake Hotel where I would be staying for a few days. I was very anxious and hesitant as I saw a lot of people carrying signs. I finally saw a huge, tall man with a turban on his head holding a sign reading "Carmie Mullen-Donahue Show." Again I was hesitant but walked toward him. His broad, friendly grin relaxed me as he introduced himself and gave me paperwork for the Drake Hotel from the Donahue Show. His limousine took me to the Drake Hotel where I was treated like a queen-everything was there for me. I could go to the dining room or bar whenever I wanted-just put it on the guest room pad.

I had tickets for plays and went to one by myself. Naomi and her daughter went by themselves, so I didn't see much of them until show time. Six dancing grannies in their sixties or seventies performed aerobic dance routines. They were in our group, plus a stripper 55 years old. They stayed at the Drake Hotel too.

We finally arrived for the show. Our make-up was checked, we were introduced to Phil and then ushered to our seats. We were introduced to the public and then Phil interviewed all of us. One at a time we were asked all sorts of questions about our busy lives at our ages. After the program was over we had time to talk to the people in the audience, mostly about the calendar, but one person asked me if I would consider coming back to New York and do modeling for his company. Of course I was flattered but I turned it down as my family was in California and that's where I wanted to be.

The calendar fun went on for the rest of the year. So many people had seen the Donahue Show so I continued to hear from people all over the state. They also had a contest on the favorite calendar girl which ran all year. Miss January, Marlene Hanson, won first place, and Miss February-me-won second place, and a year of fun that I will never forget.

Oh yes, when I got home and got off the plane I was met by my family with t-shirts. Mine read: "I was on the Phil Donahue Show" on the front and "Sexy Grandma" on the back. Theirs read: "My Mom was on the Phil Donahue Show."

STORY FORTY-SEVEN

Friends for a Lifetime

Ken Mullen, my husband, grew up with his friend, Ed Raich, in Manchester, New Hampshire. When they were small children, Ed spoke only French and Ken English. It didn't really matter as they seemed to get along and taught each other their language. When they were older, Ed and Ken and Ken's brother Lenny liked to tumble and were invited to work out in a German men's club where they learned to do acrobatics. Their neighborhood was near a small pond that froze over in the winter time where they learned to ice skate. They put ice skating together with gymnastics (or acrobatics in those days). They would skate fast toward the end of the pond where high snow banks would have formed from shoveling snow off after a snowstorm. They would flip into the air, landing in the snow bank, learning lots of different tricks, including a back flip on ice. Len joined them sometimes and they would put on shows to entertain their friends and neighbors. In high school, they participated in different sports like football, basketball, swimming and diving. After they graduated, they went their own ways.

It was a rough time for their families as the depression was on and everyone had to work and make money to feed the families and pay the bills. There were seven kids in Ken's family and about the same in Ed's. Ken found a job at the Union Leader where he set the print for the newspaper, and Ed became a clown in a traveling circus.

A few years later in Manchester, Ken and Ed got together again with Lenny and put together an acrobatic act for ice skating and called it the Hub Trio. They auditioned for the Ice Capades ice skating show which was in Boston, Massachusetts. They traveled with the show until World War II came along and the three guys were drafted into the service. They all served during the war and when they came out they rejoined the Ice Capades. Ed had been stationed in the navy in San Francisco where he met a girl named Voline at the ice rink. They were married and she joined the Ice Capades with Ed. In the meantime, I, Carmie Stewart, had been skating with the Ice Capades for four years and so had Elinor Molina, who was a singer in the show with her two sisters, also traveling with the Capades. Kenny and Lenny returned and the Hub Trio was back skating together again. Lenny fell in love with Elinor and they were married in Los Angeles. I had dated Ken for about a month then married him while we were on vacation at my home in Michigan. We six got along very well and sometimes roomed together in the same apartments or hotels. Lenny and Elinor soon had a baby named Barbara and after a year or so they left the show. Ken and Ed skated together as the Hub Duo for a few more years. Ed and Voline had a son, David, and a few months later Ken and I had our son Jim. We decided to leave the ice show.

Ken and Ed were still close buddies and decided to build a gym together in Fresno, California. It was called the M & R Health Club. They had to renovate an old building that had been a men's club. There was an unused swimming pool running wild with two-inch cockroaches, and old steam room, a dressing room, a massage room, and two handball courts. They had to knock out a couple of walls to make a big room with mats for tumbling and gym equipment. Ken and Ed spent all our savings on the club. Remembering how their parents had to struggle to pay off all their grocery bills and other charge accounts during the depression and being in debt all of the time, Ken and Ed decided to pay cash for everything. The club was doing great but the old equipment kept breaking down. The boiler on the old furnace needed help and the four of us were working day and night and raising two toddlers. Ken and Ed were the masseurs. We had no air conditioning—only a water cooler in the window. The summers were hot, especially in the car as we had to drive with the front window open. We had to signal with our elbow bent and hand raised high to turn right, out straight to turn left and straight down when we stopped. After about three years Ken and Ed were asked to go back to the Ice Capades for another tour and the money sounded good. Ken contacted Harold Zinkin who had a gym in L.A. to come and run the M & R Club for us for a year. Ken knew Harold as they had been in the service together during World War II. He said he would so we four were skating again. After a year Harold wanted to buy the gym. We were happy skating so we sold the gym and rented our homes.

Ed and Voline had their second child, Bobby, and I was pregnant with Deby and our older boys were five and needed to start school. We decided to come back to Fresno.

This time Ed and Voline started a restaurant called Pierre's and Ken became the catering manager at the Hacienda Hotel. Ed and Voline had their third child, Claudette, and later we had our third child Kathy. Ken and Ed went their own ways with their family and Ken and I too. We still got together often. Jim and Dave were in the same grade school and our Deby and their Claudette were blood sisters—yes they pricked their fingers and mixed their blood. Ken and I and Ed and Voline joined the Gem and Mineral Rock Club together when the kids were older. We were close friends until Ken's death in 1985. I would see Ed and Voline off and on until Voline's death. Then Ed would visit every once in a while. We even went to an Ice Capades reunion when we were both in our eighties! Ed is gone now so he and Ken and Lenny are back together again. They were friends for their entire lifetime!

STORY FORTY-EIGHT

Make Do

When I was a child in the late 1920's and 1930's, our families were happy to have food, clothing and shelter. We had plenty of water with our springs, rivers and lakes which were clean and fresh. We were taught if water was trickling or moving forward over rocks or sand, it was clean enough to drink. A water pump probably had a dipper or tin cup hanging on it that anyone could drink from whether he was a hobo, a stranger, or friend. We didn't worry about catching germs from them. We just shared what little we had with our neighbors, no matter who they were.

Most families lived off the land. We planted our vegetable garden and ate wild berries or fruit off our trees, caught our fish in creeks, lakes and streams and shot or trapped wild birds and small animals, even deer or bear for meat. We had a cow or two for milk and butter. We might have a flock of chickens and a rooster for eggs or eating, and a litter of pigs which had to be fed. Our parents took some of these to our little grocery store to barter or trade for staples like flour, sugar, salt, seeds or feed for our animals.We also sold some to the store for cash to buy some cloth for clothing. My brother would set traps in the woods for rabbits, foxes and other small animals for their meat and would also sell their fur for cash.

We had to sew our own clothes which were possibly made from flour sacks or gunny sacks. You wore the same clothing all year and then passed it down to the younger child as you grew out of it or as the younger child grew into it. When clothing wore out it went to the rag bag which was torn into strips for bandages or crocheted into rugs for the floor. The same with old sheets –when they were worn out in the center they were torn in half lengthwise and sewn with the outsides together with the center now on the outside edges. Now you can "make do" for a while longer. Old sheets were torn to make towels, bandages, or stripped and rolled into balls to be crocheted into rugs or mats. They were also torn into strips for sanitary napkins to be worn pinned to a sanitary belt during a girl's menstrual cycle.

As Dad worked himself up in the lumber business he moved his family into town. We kids were able to go to the regular schools instead of a one room school for all ages and Mom began to make extra money as a seamstress making clothes for the public. We were able to afford a washing machine and had running water inside our home. We were still "making do" with our one pair of shoes each a year for each child. When the sole of a shoe came loose and formed a flapper, Dad would simply cut the flapper off and patch it with a rubber sole made out of a piece of an old tire tube. If a shoe had a hole worn in the bottom, Dad would "make do" with sticking a cardboard or rubber sole inside the shoe.

It was hard for our families during the 1930's and the Great Depression. Again my dad moved us to a better home in a better neighborhood. My mother was now helping with the bills by doing the laundry for all the lumberjacks at Dad's camp, and she was still sewing for the public too. My brother and sisters were in high school so they had to help out. Loretta had quit school so our mom gave her the job of cooking and cleaning our new house. Ella helped Mom with sewing and my brother was helping Dad on weekends with his bookkeeping in a logging camp, and Viva was babysitting for other families and setting hair for a few ladies. Dad and Reinard Hemkes (who married Loretta and was a carpenter) built a new house for us. It had all the ex-tras like bathroom with tub and laundry room with hot and cold running water, and electric lights. Ella moved down to Detroit to a beauty and modeling school. Sterl was off to Indiana University and Viva was off to Grand Rapids to a business school. I was home finishing high school and helping Mom with renting out the empty rooms to tourists that came to our town to visit our famous Tahquamenon Falls. My job was to clean and dust the rooms and change the beds every day. I also had to wash the sheets, hang them outside to dry and iron them with a mangle, which was a long rolling three foot iron for ironing sheets. We also served juice, bacon, eggs, toast and coffee every day. It came with the bedroom. By now we had everything we needed and rarely had to "make do"—we had an indoor bathroom, indoor hot and cold water, faucets, electric lights, plenty of store-bought sheets, clothes, shoes when needed, refrigerator, electric or gas stoves and much, much more! They were the best hard-working and loving parents ever!

STORY FORTY-NINE

Outhouses, Glopjars and Bushes

When I was a little girl about three years old in 1924 we had moved from Onaway, Michigan, where Dad and Mom were farmers, to Newberry, Michigan, which was in the Upper Peninsula forests. We moved in with Dad's sister, Aunt Ella, and my Uncle Mack McTiver. Uncle Mack lived on the farm but also was in charge of a lumber camp nearby. Dad started working in the camps and loved the work and became a lumberjack. We stayed with them until we found a little shack closer to town on the Tahquamenon River. We were very crowded with our relatives. We had five kids in our family and they had five too. They had an outhouse outside their home which they called their "privy". An outhouse is a small building containing a bench with two or three holes cut into it for people to sit on. The building sat over a deep hole in the ground. It was the family toilet and was moved every couple of years and then the hole was covered over. It usually contained a Sears or Montgomery Ward's catalog for toilet paper. Most homes had an outhouse in their back yard.

Our new home had a "two-holer" in the back but we had lots of bushes and trees for the kids to play hide and seek or squat behind. My mom always had a slop jar on the floor at the foot of their bed. It was a granite pail with a cover which could be used at night when it was too cold and dark to go outside. My sisters and brother had been walking to a one room schoolhouse and I was old enough to start kindergarten so we again moved into town closer to a regular school. Dad and Mom found a two family house. We were in the front half and another family, the Sorensons, lived in the back. There was a long covered porch on the far side of the house from the front to the back with an outhouse at the end to share with both families. It was really great in the wintertime because we didn't have to run outside to use the outhouse in the cold snow. When I was about twelve years old we moved even closer to the school in the town of Newberry. We had a real indoor bathroom upstairs where our bedrooms were. We not only had a real toilet but a bathtub too and a hanging electric light instead of a gas or kerosene lamp. What a luxury! There weren't too many public bathrooms in town so if we drove our car to another town we were always stopping at a bush to hide behind for a "potty break"—boys to the left of the road and girls to the right.

Here it is eighty years later and people are still coming up with new ideas for outdoor conveniences. My son-in-law, Steve, takes a folding hospital potty chair when he goes camping. He digs a hole in the woods in back of his tent, sets the chair over the hole that he dug, and has his perfect throne! Slop jars, outhouses, portable potty chairs or trees and bushes—a person's gotta do what a person's gotta do to go doo! What did you do?

STORY FIFTY

Summer Woes

Early this summer while doing aquatics at the BTB swimming pool my knee seemed to pop and give way as I entered the water. It hurt like crazy—I'm sure I would have fallen if I hadn't been in the water. I floated on a water noodle the rest of the class. I drove myself home bit my left side really hurt. I couldn't stand any more. I called my daughter and she came home with a wheelchair in the back of her truck and took me to my doctor. He checked me, took x-rays, and then sent me home with orders to stay flat in bed for four days. It seems like "Arthur" has found a home in my lower back causing my leg to be weak and sore. I still take therapy in the water with the aid of a water noodle and my coach helps me to get up and down steps. I'm not allowed to go in and out of our pool at home without some-one else in the pool with me. I also walk with a cane as my gait and balance is not secure.

One day I was at home alone and had been watering our plants and flowers when I noticed that the steps going into the pool and the bench seats in the pool on either side of the diving board needed sweeping. I'd swept them millions of times before so I just picked up the long pipe with a brush on the end and pushed the dust off the steps and then continued on to the deep end. I walked around chairs, tables, lounges, and umbrellas. I stepped carefully up one step to the pool deck, walked around the diving board three or four feet away from the pool edge and carefully stepped down the one step to the lower deck again. I was watching my step down, but not the pipe push broom I was carrying which all of a sudden hit one of the chairs at the side of the pool and knocked me back through the air, dumping me into the deep end of the pool. What a surprise! I swam up and out to the edge of the pool where I found the seat that I was supposed to sweep. I could sit on it but couldn't climb up and out of the pool. I couldn't lift my knee up high enough. I was stuck! I couldn't get out! Panic! I looked around. I was alone. All my family and neighbors were working. It was so quiet—should I shout? I looked in the pool. The push broom was near and my sandals were floating. I fished them out with the broom. I was able to put my sandals up on the deck, put my forearms and elbows on each shoe and literally lifted my weight until I could get a knee under me to grab a chair leg and pull myself up to safety. Wow!

Later on my daughter, Deby, said: "Mom, why didn't you just walk your hands along the top of the pool? You were so close for your feet to touch the bottom and you could just walk out."

Smart punk!!! Oh to be young again!!!

STORY FIFTY-ONE

The Art Linkletter Show

Kids say the darndest things! In 1961, our daughter Deby was in the first grade at John Muir Elementary School. Four of the students, two boys and two girls, were chosen to be on the Art Linkletter Show—Deby, Anna Kreuter, Richard Penner and another boy named Joe. Their families and ours were to drive to Hollywood on Friday. The Art Linkletter Show would put us in a hotel Friday night and then we would meet with them at the studio in the morning to discuss the show. The cameras would roll live in the afternoon in front of a big studio audience. Ken and I decided to go and take Jim with us and leave Kathy, our baby, with our friend and babysitter, Beverly May. Deby had taken dance lessons since she was two years old, so she was so excited to be on stage!

The day arrived and we took off for Hollywood in our station wagon. Wouldn't you know it started to snow as we started to drive over The Grapevine—a pass through the hills that lead into Los Angeles. We had car trouble and limped into a mechanic's garage where they looked for the trouble!

They told us we needed a part that they had to order and it wouldn't come in until Monday. We ended up finding a motel room in Gorman that night and caught a bus to Hollywood the next morning, leaving our car in Gorman.

We made it to our morning meeting where we joined our other friends and their kids. The kids were asked a lot of personal questions like where their parents met, where they worked, etc. In the afternoon when they shot the show Art Linkletter asked the kids the questions asked previously. When it came to Deby he asked, "What is Fresno famous for?" Deby remembered the questions earlier and thought about the "where did your dad work" so her answer was—Fresno is famous for the Hacienda Hotel. The audience laughed so Art Linkletter said "Wow, that's good advertising at work." They laughed again. Then he asked, "How did your Mom and Dad meet?" Deby answered, "They were skating with Ice Capades and when they were skating they bumped into each other." He asked, "So they fell for each other?" Deby nodded yes. He said, "That's a cold start of a love affair!" The audience laughed and laughed. The other kids were asked the same questions. Some were quiet and shy or loud and funny. Art Linkletter was great with the kids.

For being on the show, the children were each given a shiny new Red Flyer wagon, a portable record player, and a hatbox full of bubble bath, paper dolls and coloring books. And they had lunch with Art Linkletter at the famous Brown Derby restaurant. We had to carry all the "Big Prizes" to the bus station and the driver had to stuff them in his baggage compartment. We rode back to Gorman for our car, it still was not fixed, so we called AAA.

It was a fun but hectic trip! To keep this great memory alive, The Art Linkletter Show gave all of the kids a recording on a record of the whole "Kids say the darndest things" interview to play on their new record player and an 8 X 10 picture of them on the show with Art Linkletter. It was quite an adventure—snow, broken-down car, bus ride, fancy hotel, TV interview, lunch at a famous "Hollywood Brown Derby" restaurant, car towed home. And when we asked Deby what she enjoyed most, she said, "The bubble bath that turns the water different colors." "Kids DO say the darndest things!"

STORY FIFTY-TWO

Grapes to Raisins

When Deby and Steve were first married, Steve's grandparents hired Steve to care for their twenty-acre vineyard. It also had a nice ranch house and four huge black walnut trees. As a teenager, Steve helped his grandfather, his relatives, and the workers. Each year they had to follow a certain process to grow grapes and turn them into raisins. It was new to Deby but she loved the ranch life, especially because she was with the love of her life—Steven. They had lots of wild rabbits to tame, three or four dogs and cats to enjoy plus many puppies and kittens that they found homes for.

They had to irrigate the old vines and then prune them, leaving five or six vines on each plant to be stretched and tied to a wire in each direction. As the grapes grew, Steve had to plow and disc and furrow the land for irrigation, then finally smooth and flatten the land to get ready for picking. The new foliage would produce bunches of grapes hanging down under the vines. In August the bunches had to be cut with a sharp knife and laid on papers which had been placed on the ground between the rows. If it rained the water would puddle in the holes under the papers causing the grapes to mildew. If the papers and grapes get wet the papers need to be lifted by the corners and quickly slid a couple of inches to break the suction under the paper tray. When the bunches of grapes get dry in the hot central California sun they turn into raisins. The papers are rolled into bundles and placed close to the vines. As the tractor moves down the rows pulling a trailer the workers pick up the bundles and stack on the trailer. The tractor takes the raisins over to the long, slanted shaker table.

The raisins are dumped from the paper trays onto the shaker table which has been turned on, and papers are tossed on the side to be burned later as the raisins travel down the wire mesh-based shaker table. The whole table shakes as the raisins roll down and the workers stand on either side, picking out the rot, the dirt clods, stems and leaves. The raisins fall into huge bins which are lifted by a forklift and stacked on the big diesel truck to be delivered to the wineries. The raisins are processed and boxed to sell in the stores. Their raisins became "Sun Maid Raisins".

What I liked best was—I was a teacher's aide with the Fresno County Schools and we were invited to take our 10 to 12-year-old students on several field trips to the ranch. We picked up black walnuts that had fallen under the trees. We cracked them and ate them. Our students were able to keep what they picked up. Steve and Deb gave us a couple of rolls of raisins that were fresh from the field.

At school our students picked out the rot and stems and washed them. The next day, Dolly Trout, our teacher, and the students learned to make black walnut and raisin cookies. We ate some and took the rest to the ranch and gave them to Deby and Steve as a "thank you" for teaching us so much about the grapes to raisins process.